Buy and ~~*Hold*~~ Hope

How I Beat the Pros, Doubled the Nasdaq, Spending ONLY 1 Minute-a-week

Randall Mauro

ISBN-13: 978-1499245820

ISBN-10: 1499245823

It should not be assumed that the methods, techniques, or indicators presented in this book will be profitable or that they will not result in losses. Past results are not necessarily indicative of future results. Examples in this book are for educational purposes only. This is not a solicitation of any order to buy or sell.

The National Futures Association (NFA) requires us to state that "Hypothetical or simulated performance results have certain inherent limitations. Unlike an actual performance record, simulated results do not represent actual trading. Also, since the trades have not actually been executed, the results may have under or over compensated for the impact, if any, of certain market factors, such as lack of liquidity. Simulated trading programs in general are also subject to the fact that they are designed with the benefit of hindsight. No representation is being made that any account will or is likely to achieve profits or losses similar to these shown."

A Very Special Thank You

RESNN … What can I say about RESNN, they are my life … my everything.

E – thank you for supporting my decision to walk away from a successful business in Los Angeles to pursue my dreams, for being understanding when 'I never make it to dinner on time', and for not falling asleep while 'talking stock' with me. You're a trooper! But, most of all, thank you for your beautiful smile and for giving me my purpose. We make a great team you and I.

S and N – thank you for keeping me laughing and for your understanding when you just want to 'dog pile on the daddy' and I'm tired and cranky.

And … N – You impress me more than you'll ever know. I am VERY proud of you and crazy excited to see what you make of your future. When's your first book coming out? I'm serious when I tell you that you are a MUCH better writer than I could ever dream of being. The world will miss out if you they don't get to see your words. You've got so much passion in you … get it down on paper. I took the first step, now it's your turn…

"Everyone has the brainpower

to follow the stock market.

If you made it through fifth-grade math,

you can do it."

Peter Lynch

An Introduction

"Money can't buy happiness, but neither can Poverty." *– Leo Rosten*

I discovered what I am about to share with you roughly 10 years ago and have been investing my own money solely using this approach since then. Over those 10 years, my worst performing year resulted in a loss of less than 7%, while the average investor's worst year resulted in a loss of over 40%.

In fact, over the last 40 years, this technique never had a single year of double digit losses; its' worst performing year was in 1984 with a loss a 9.9%. I want to repeat that ... imagine losing less than 10% while all your friends were losing almost half of their worth (multiple times)!! Looking at the chart below, you can see the NASDAQ's 5 worst performing years and how we compare. What a difference!

	Us	Nasdaq	Difference
2008	-4.50%	-40.50%	36.00%
2002	-7.90%	-31.50%	23.70%
2001	6.50%	-21.10%	27.60%
2000	-9.20%	-39.30%	30.10%
1990	6.60%	-17.80%	24.40%

You see, most people have it all wrong when it comes to stock market investing. For starters, they chase performance trying to find the next big winner focusing on profit *potential*, but what you will find after reading this book is that true wealth is not achieved by trying to find the next big winner but rather by trying to avoid the next major decline. *Long-term Success in the stock market is not determined by how well you do in the good times, but rather how less bad you do in the bad times.*

"The best offense is a good defense." *– Mao Zedong*

Corrections happen, and focusing on avoiding these declines makes the difference between retiring with buckets full of money and just getting by. By emphasizing capital preservation (not losing what you have) instead of growth, you will do better than 99.9% of all investors out there. In fact, the strategy has more than doubled the return of the average investor; 225% better than a traditional 'buy and hold' approach.

But wait … it gets even better … As I mentioned earlier, most people have it all wrong … they think in order to have a chance of beating the averages they need to devote all their time to learning the nuances of the market and watching its' every tick. This just isn't so. In fact, I found that in most instances, the more you micromanage your account, the worse your performance generally is. If you want to learn to day trade or actively trade, this is NOT the book for you. This book is for people that want a simple technique that is intended to keep you safe in volatile times, to protect their investments, have it grow nicely and go on living their life.

"Your time is limited, so don't waste it …" *– Steve Jobs*

Amazingly as you will see, it involves **only 1 minute-a-week, 20 seconds-a-day** … and more importantly it doesn't require a PHD in Quantitative Analysis or any formal education whatsoever. Better still, you don't need to learn some fancy trading algorithm or use a risky or complex product like futures or derivatives. If you are smart enough to open an account at your brokerage firm then you have all the smarts you need to protect yourself from future declines.

I feel strongly that there is no safer way to invest in the stock market, and quite honestly no better way. The performance speaks for itself; in fact I have blown the doors off of virtually all other investing approaches out there. Sound too good to be true? It isn't. The information I intend to show you is NOT opinion, it is FACT. I provide all evidence herein for you to validate.

By the end of this book, you will very defiantly agree that 'buy and ~~*hold*~~ hope' is NOT the best way to invest, not by a long shot. There is a better way, and there is only one person that can stop the next decline from affecting your future, and that is you. As you'll see here, it doesn't take more than a few minutes of time, but you have to do it. Complacency has no place in the investment world.

> ***"A pessimist complains about the wind; an optimist expects it to change; the realist adjusts the sails"*** - *W. A. Ward*

My name is Randall Mauro and this is my story. My background is quite different than most in the financial world. In fact, I never aspired to work in the industry and consider myself an outsider when talking to other financial planners, advisors or brokers. My journey has been very different, mostly because I don't have the best image of Wall Street. I arrived here quite frankly out of disgust of the way things were and still are, and had a desire to find a better way.

I am a Registered Investment Advisor (RIA), the CEO and Chief Investment Officer of Resnn Investments, LLC, a money management firm that invests money in the stock market in a very protective manner. From January 1st 2008 through December 31st 2012 (a period of 5 years), our investment at Resnn has more than doubled, returning 129% vs. the S&P500 returning only 8.6%. We did this while reducing risk exponentially from a traditional 'buy and hold' investment. As an example in 2008 we lost only 3.6% while the S&P lost 36.8%. If you had 1 million dollars invested, that is the difference of more than $330,000.00 in one year.

If you had earned $330,000 more last year, would that be helpful toward your financial goals? You bet it would!

$330,000 would buy a nice house in Denver (where I live), pay for 4 years tuition at Harvard or Yale (with room and board), a Lamborghini Murcielago (but not the cost to insure it), a vacation condo in the ski town of Steamboat Springs, CO, or maybe a flawless 3 ½ carat diamond ring (or not so flawless 7.5 carats). This is just one year's difference … imagine if you were able to do this every few years. Just think of the possibilities. As you will see with examples later on, we are not talking about small differences here. This is the difference between having an average retirement and being able to do anything you want in retirement.

There is a better way to invest and protect your money, and this book will give you the tools to achieve it. In fact, I opened Resnn because I realized that this strategy, which I created years ago for my own investments is truly phenomenal and quite honestly too good to keep to myself. But first let me be perfectly clear … I don't need your money. I'm not writing this book for money, I don't have a stock picking subscription service, I don't host seminars that I charge for … I have no need to do business with you or anyone else for that matter.

My goal in writing this book is to share my experience (both good and bad) with you and to hopefully help you avoid the pain that I went through on my own eye-opening journey. And if you are so inclined to take matters in your own hands, which I encourage, I hope to give you some very real, verifiable and most importantly, easy-to-use techniques to substantially beat the market; to protect your hard earned nest egg consistently and reliably.

> ***"It is not the strongest of the species that survive, nor the most intelligent, but the ones most responsive to change."*** - *Charles Darwin*

Now, a word of caution … I know that some will read this book and not be able to achieve what I have, not because it is difficult (in fact quite the opposite) but simply because of what I mentioned above … that most people have it all wrong when it comes to investing in the market. In fact, I bet a few of you read the page above and saw "this book is for people that want a *SIMPLE* technique," and instantly felt that this isn't the right book for you … a successful strategy that more than doubles the average return while reducing risk exponentially couldn't possibly be *simple* … or could it?

The biggest challenge we have ahead of us is not in learning some tough trading algorithm but in trying to retrain our way of thinking; to look at things differently than we previously have. It involves you being open to non-traditional investing ideas, and to challenge the status quo. Listen … you picked up this book for a reason, and I bet it is out of frustration and desire to change the way you currently invest in the market. I know that's how I started my journey. So, please keep an open mind as you read the contents herein, and I'm certain you will be pleased with the outcome.

> ***"An investment in knowledge pays the best interest."*** – *Ben Franklin*

I hope you enjoy the journey, but more so I hope that you embrace what I shared above … take charge of your destiny as I have. Be the captain of your own ship and never again be at the mercy of the market.

Prologue

"One evening, while having dinner with a fundamentalist, I accidentally knocked a sharp knife off the edge of the table. He watched the knife twirl through the air, as it came to rest with the pointed end sticking into his shoe. 'Why didn't you move your foot?' I exclaimed. 'I was waiting for it to come back up,' he replied." - *Ed Seykota*

In 2008, the average investor lost over 45% of their net worth in just 3 months … for every $1.00 they had in the market, it was now only 55 cents. $1 million became $550,000. Some say the 'Great Recession of 2008' was more painful than any other recession, **but it wasn't**.

2008 hit us all hard (mentally and financially) only because it was so recent for all of us. The human brain is conditioned to remember and act on recent pain more than pain from a long time ago. It is a survival mechanism that dates back to our cave man days. Yet for survival in the stock market it is imperative to remember all the facts to help us to know what is normal and what is not. And unfortunately, looking over history, what we see is that **2008 was not abnormal**.

The reality is that massive loss occurs and occurs often. In fact, there has never been a period of more than a few years where *peace* and *calmness* was a reality for our investments in the market. I was born in 1970. Looking at my life time alone we see that every 2-5 years there was substantial loss in value.

- In 1973 the market lost over 60% of its' value, and took until mid 1979 to break-even.
- In 1978 we had a 2 month nasty drop of over 20%.

- Two years later, in February 1980 we had another 2 month scare where the market lost 25%.
- One year after that, in May 1981 we had a 25% decline.
- Then came Black Monday in October 1987, where we saw a 36% drop over 2 months, with over 20% of the loss occurring in just 2 days!
- 3 years later, August 1990 the market dropped over 30% in 2 months.
- June 1996 the market dropped over 16.5% in one month.
- August 1998 through October 1998, 2.5 months … 30% drop.
- From 2000 to 2003 the average NASDAQ mutual fund lost 78% of its' value, and has yet to come close to break-even as I write this 13 years later.
- 2008 the average investor lost over 45% in 3 months.
- April 2010 through July 2010 17% + loss over 3 months.
- One year later, another 18% + drop that lasted from April through October 2011.

2008 wasn't a game changer in any way. It was no different than any other correction listed above. We **WILL** have another 2008 … the cause might be different, but the loss in value, the pain … won't be.

The reason for the declines vary from the government altering the Federal Funds Rate to deal with Inflation, computer glitches, banking fiasco's, tsunami's, floods, nuclear disasters, multiple wars and terror attacks … **but the reasons don't really matter**. What matters is the outcome … the loss, the pain, the years of lost savings that now need to be recouped.

Prologue

"The United States has developed a new weapon that destroys people but it leaves buildings standing. It's called the stock market." *- Jay Leno*

There will ALWAYS be some *reason* for panic to appear in the market, and trying to guess why or when the next one will occur is a fool's errand, but … protecting yourself from these massive drops in value is a very real issue. Coming up with a game plan for how to deal with the next impending financial crisis is what separates the super affluent from the rest of the world.

We have been taught mostly by the big brokerage and mutual firms to *'buy and hold;'* to trust that "the market always goes up," but the reality is that at a certain stage in our life we don't have the leisure to *trust* that everything will recover. Looking over history, the average time to get back to break-even after a decline is between 2 and 5 years (although we have yet to recoup from the losses of 2000, 14years later). **Can you afford to wait 2 - 14 + years just to break-even on your investments when we have another situation like the dot-com bubble?**

Wouldn't it be amazing if instead of just trying to get back to break-even you could avoid these large declines and not lose sleep at night trying to figure out whether you will need to postpone retirement OR change your spending habits to accommodate your lost net worth?

Are you ready for another 2008? **BE HONEST WITH YOURSELF, are you ready?** Because it WILL happen. It's not a question of if 2008 will happen again; it is simply a question of when. Don't fool yourself into thinking that 2008 was an anomaly. News commentators love to imply that the *current situation* is more treacherous than all the previous ones. You hear a lot of "this time it is different" as the declines happen. The truth though, is that history is full of "*this time it's different's*" and yet the declines still come and wipe away years of savings.

> ***"The four most dangerous words in investing are: 'This time it's different'"*** *– Sir John Templeton*

I want to repeat this important point … news happens, disasters happen, government's meddle … the reason for the *bad news* doesn't matter, **the only thing that matters is the impact these events have on your bank account**, and history has shown us that the next large decline won't be far off … 2 – 5 years at most.

Nothing has changed since 2008, the system hasn't gotten safer, no safeguards have been imposed to protect from another decline. Yet Wall Street is hopeful that as time goes on we will all fall asleep at the wheel again … *Buying and Hoping.*

My purpose here is not to scare you, or to try to predict the next 'perfect storm' but rather to prepare you for the inevitable. Like any disaster, the more prepared you are, the more likely you will get through it with little to no pain.

> ***"The stock market is never obvious. It is designed to fool most of the people, most of the time."*** *– Jesse Livermore*

Don't waste energy trying to understand the impact of some news event, just be prepared for the worst case scenario and when that day comes you will be ready for it … it's that simple.

I learned a long time ago that there isn't a lot of sense to the market, and the sooner you realize this the better your performance will be. Don't fixate on the when, why, what and where … just focus on *how* to protect your portfolio IF 'the what' causes a negative impact. I'll give you the tools to do this later on, but know that you don't have to pay big time analysts or read fancy broker reports to be able to protect yourself. It will take you literally 1 minute-a-week to know what to do next.

By the way, I have listed only the 'big drops' in market value at the start of this chapter. I'm not including the small ones (between 5 and 15%) that occur two to three times a year because the list above would be massive. But know that corrections happen, and they happen often … and by the time you are finished with this book, you will be ready to proactively deal with the next one that comes your way regardless of what news created it.

PART I

Buying and Hoping

It was a Saturday in late February 2004. Tax time … and I was getting my financial statements together to go to my accountant the following week.

I remember looking over my investments and specifically a 401k statement when I suddenly realized that I hadn't made a dime in about 10 years! I remember feeling sick to my stomach as I walked to the garage to dig out some old financial statements to verify my findings. **This couldn't be … not one dime in 10 years???** Come on, we had just been through one of the greatest tech booms in the history of mankind, and I didn't profit from it??

It's been a long, arduous journey to arrive to today; many frustrating days that I now realize had a purpose to help me learn that there is a better way. I hope my stories, my *lessons* in Part I help you to avoid some of the pitfalls on your journey that I had to experience on mine.

Chapter 1

You Would Not Believe the Week I've had ...

I nodded my head in agreement, although I was biting my tongue as he spoke. I remember looking across at him, across the oversized mahogany desk in his opulent office in the heart of Beverly Hills, CA. For a moment, I mentally left the conversation as I looked out the floor to ceiling windows, taking in his view of downtown Beverly Hills and further off in the distance the Hollywood Hills and even the HOLLYWOOD sign. It was truly a magnificent view, definitely one of the better views in Los Angeles and quite fitting for him.

I was sitting in the office of one of the wealthiest, most successful music managers in the entertainment industry. Being early in my career I knew that this meeting was as important as they come. Getting him as a client could push our firm up a notch in the food chain which is something I worked incredibly hard to make happen. In fact, this meeting hadn't happened by chance but by months of hustle to catch the eye of one man whom I was now sitting across from.

It was hard to keep my mouth shut … sure he had a tough week, heck his name was plastered across every news publication in the world. A PR nightmare for sure but I had just experienced one of the few moments in life that truly changes the rest of it. A life altering moment in the truest sense of the word.

My first born son was born on April 6, 1998. If you've been lucky enough to have children and even more lucky to be in the room while your wife delivers the baby or babies (more on this later) you will agree that this is one of life's most precious moments. Although the months after this day were quite a blur with sleep deprivation that I now fondly call, *The Fog of War*, this day will always be firmly seated in my memory.

I remember many things about that day, but what I remember most is how complete I felt in that hospital room with my wife sleeping (recovering) and myself looking over our newborn child. It was the middle of the night and an amazingly peaceful evening (especially considering we were inside a hospital). My son, whose is now (at the time of this writing) a perfect stereotypical 15-year-old; perfect in the sense that he is obnoxious, rude and continually amazing me with the stupidity that comes out of his mouth on a daily basis (just kidding N!!), was fussing in the bassinet and I was standing over him watching and trying to make sense of all that had occurred over the past 12 hours.

At that moment, I was swept over with a sense of calm … I realized that everything that I had searched for up to that point really didn't matter. A sense of clarity washed over me as I realized my entire life's work, all my possessions, all the clients that I had worked so hard to please over the past few years; none of it mattered. I realized that in that teeny hospital room, I had everything I had needed and will ever need to feel complete. The clothes on my back, a toothbrush, and the two other beings in that room, nothing else mattered or ever will matter more.

This realization hits all of us new parents at different times, most in the first few months, some … it takes years to figure out, but there really is nothing better than your first child to help you to realize what really matters in this world and what *the purpose of life* is. You see, for me and most men, we spend most of our lives searching for that *purpose*, trying to find meaning in our existence. Sadly, many of us never find it as we continue to spend our lives searching, yet I was lucky enough to be hit on the head that wonderful evening.

I was filled with so many emotions that peaceful evening as I stood over my new child and looked longingly over at my beautiful wife sleeping, pondering deep questions as I mentioned above, but inevitably as a guy the topic in your head always, always heads in one direction. This evening was no different. You guys know what this is, any woman in the audience that are along for the ride might not be certain but I'll give you one guess at the question rolling around in my head … and NOOO

Elizabeth (my wife) I wasn't thinking of anything perverted, jeez … I mean I just watched the creation of life, I think I could pause that emotion for a day or two at least. :)

So what was the deep question that I was pondering, guys? Call me a selfish jerk, but I can't deny what I was pondering. Give up? Ok, here goes …

HOW MUCH IS THIS GOING TO COST ME???

Listen, maybe it's a fault of mine, but one thing you'll discover about me is that I'm brutally honest. The mathematics here were/are astounding … 2 suddenly became 3 and somehow that third being although only ¼ of the size of the other two in the house accounted for ¾ of the spending habits that would ensue over the coming years. *Funny Math* for sure!

My son's birth would forever change my life for many reasons, but one in particular took roughly 10 years to play out before I realized it. My mom on that day gifted my son, her new grandson, $10,000.00 of Sun MicroSystems stock. Remember this was 1998 and as you probably experienced yourself or if you were too young to know, the next year and a half was a wild time for the stock market to say the least. Some say what we experienced will never occur again in the history of mankind but in the investing world the first rule that you learn is to *never say never*. Suffice to say, the dot-com bubble *ride* was a fun time for dreamers.

Fast forward two years … mid 2000. As a parent you know what those 2 years bring, a whole lot of fun and more *awakenings* on the meaning of life. After only owning Sun Microsystems for these two years his stock was now worth over $265,000.00 … a <u>2,550% gain</u> … wow! Can you imagine!

To put this in perspective, if you had invested $10,000.00 in the Nasdaq 33 years ago (in 1981), it would now be worth a little over $200,000.00 using a simple 'buy and hold' strategy. This was / is an impressive 2000% return, but what typically took over 30+ years took only 2 years during the dot-com bubble.

I remember sitting down with my wife one Saturday evening and looking over the brokerage statement. We were ecstatic to say the least. His college was easily paid for, and at this rate he would have been worth more than us by the time he was 4. We pondered selling some of his stock but as I mentioned … it was a good time for dreamers. We decided to 'buy and ~~*hold*~~ hope'.

We all know the ending of this story and I'm sure most of you have a similar story to tell. We sold his stock a few years later for $4,000.00 (a loss of $6,000.00). Yes, you read right … 4k.

Ugh … How did we go from a gain of $265,000.00 to a loss of $6,000.00?? Well, it took me a few years to understand this and now in hind sight I know this was a very INEXPENSIVE lesson given what I now know (I'm getting ahead of myself, but you heard right … Inexpensive. More on this later in the story)

So … how did we make such a bumbling error and hold the stock for as long as we did? One word … Life. We all are busy and as you know … the more *successful* you are the busier life seems to be. We don't have time to watch every movement of the tape. Life is just too busy.

For me, my focus was on the role of CEO at my consulting firm in Los Angeles. We had started the company only a few years earlier but had immediate success which I document in my upcoming book, *Consultant to the Stars: Business Lessons from a Geek on the Wall.* The dot-com boom was a double edged sword for our business but suffice to say I was very busy growing the company and focusing all my effort on the day-to-day operational details of the business.

In fact, we as investors love the concept of 'buy and hold', because it takes no time to manage. You get to experience the thrill of buying something, that newness smell, enjoying the sexiness of whatever life altering thing this company does (i.e. *sexy* in the stock market currently means: 3d printing, creating space tourism and trains that can take you across the United States in a few hours inside a vacuum), kicking the tires and then the best part is dreaming about your future riches while you pat yourself on the back about how smart you are.

But **how does this outcome usually end up?** Once the newness wears off we get busy with life again; it just takes too much work to manage our portfolio and so 'buy and hold' usually becomes 'buy and hope'.

As a side note that I will dig into deeper in my upcoming book, *Trust, but Verify*, our brokers and financial advisors love this about us. In fact they hope to lull us into a state of complacency falling asleep at the wheel or worse letting someone else be the captain of our ship that isn't qualified to do so.

> ***"... people spend more time analyzing washing machines than they do picking their retirement fund, even though retirement funds have much more of an impact on their quality of life."*** - *James Angel, associate finance professor at Georgetown University.*

If you had invested $10,000.00 exactly 40 years ago in the NASDAQ, it would now be worth slightly over $400,000.00 with a simple 'buy and hold' strategy. This was / is an impressive 3983% compounded return OR a little over 9.7% average annual return.

Now, let's be honest with each other ... 400k isn't going to make much of a difference in your retirement years. Don't get me wrong it's no small chunk of change but given that it took 40 years to build it's nothing to get excited over. To prove my point, let's do some math ...

First off ... if you take into account inflation (average annual inflation is 3.3%), your 10k investment actually grew to $119,000.00 (9.7% annual return less 3.3% inflation = 6.4% annual return). Technically you earned 400k, but since everything is more expensive than it was 40 years ago ... the

400k that your nest egg is now worth doesn't buy as much as it did 40 years ago. Remember that 40 years ago, $10,000 was a lot of money, in fact the average person made 10k in their annual salary. So to project how much money you have to live off, we need to include inflation into the calculations.

Next, let's assume today you retire and you are 65 years old, currently the average U.S. life expectancy is 79 years of age, this means your 119k must last 14 years more years, but what if you live to 90 or 95 (as my Grandpa did)? You obviously don't want to run out of money, so you really need to plan for a much longer life ... so let's assume you need enough income to last 25 years. This gives you $4,783 ($119k divided by 25 years) to spend each and every year of your retirement!

But wait ... during those 25 years though, let's assume you still have the money invested in the stock market, even though most investment advisors would suggest you only have a small portion in the market and most in safer, but lower yielding bonds and CDs, but let's assume the best case scenario here and assume you continue to make what you previously made (6.4% annual return after inflation). If you want the 400k to last for exactly 25 years, and each year your investment earns 6.4% you will be able to spend $33,000 each and every year (in today's dollars), until your 91st birthday at which time you will have nothing left.

We haven't even discussed the tax ramifications on your profitable investments, but I think without even doing that you see my point ... **could you survive off of $33k a year right now?** Even if you have your house paid for and you live a meager life with no travel, 33k is pretty hard to pull off. Certainly it doesn't sound like a fun way to spend your golden years. I personally hope to travel, spend time with (and spoil) my grandkids and not be too concerned with making my dollars last. For me generating wealth is about creating freedom and choice, not about greed. I want options when I'm an old fart, not to be held captive by my retirement funds.

Now what if you took the same $10,000 and put it in the same investment (NASDAQ) for the same amount of years (1973 through 2013) and by spending less than 1 minute-a-week, that same $400,000 would become over $900,000. Almost 3 times better.

Now let's say that instead of starting with $10,000 you started with $100,000 … after forty years a 'buy and hold' strategy would have returned $4 million while the strategy here would have returned over $10 million, and lastly, starting with $1 million leaves you at the end with $100 million vs. 40 million. As you can see 'buying and holding' has done quite well, but by spending just a one minute-a-week, you can blow the doors off your neighbor's performance.

Now … before you turn on the bull%@# alarm, if you keep reading I intend to show proof on how you can do this. Spending no more than 1 minute-a-week.

$10 million, now there's some real money. **Would your retirement years be a tad different if you had $10 million (or better yet … 100 million) in your nest egg?** I can tell you that when I discovered this years ago I took note and completely changed my investing approach forever.

Are you skeptical at this point?? I certainly hope so!! In fact, if you aren't, I would be willing to bet that you have little net worth because you've been huckstered time and time again to the point that you've made a lot of people rich, unfortunately just not yourself.

Being skeptical is normal (especially in the investment world), it is a learned response by being promised time and time again of untold riches and then never seeing them. I can tell you that I have been huckstered myself many times in the past, both by well intentioned individuals and huge multi-billion dollar publicly traded companies. If you knew how many hundreds of books I've read and thousands of hours (literally) that I've spent on learning the latest 'make a fortune in the stock market,' 'get rich-quick' technique, only to find after testing that 99.999% of them were a load of crock. Maybe my words here are strong, but after reading this book I have a feeling you will never look at a *retirement guide* from your brokerage or mutual fund company the same way again.

The next time you go into Home Depot and walk past the washing machines, I want you to think of $10,000,000 … and think of me, my son and his most amazing investment in Sun Microsystems. Because at the end of the day …

It really doesn't matter how much you make, it only matters how much you keep.

I know that by reading this book, you are giving me the one thing in life you cannot get more of … your time. In return, I hope that I am able to give you some very real tools to help you build substantial wealth for yourself and your loved ones … and skepticism is one of the most important of these tools. I for one will NEVER, EVER let another Sun Microsystems story happen to my investment portfolio again, and I hope in reading this book that you also will NEVER, EVER make the same mistake as well.

Chapter 2

1987

ROCK-A BYE BABY ON THE TREE TOP,

WHEN THE WIND BLOWS THE CRADLE WILL ROCK,

WHEN THE BOUGH BREAKS THE CRADLE WILL FALL,

AND DOWN WILL COME BABY ... CRADLE AND ALL!

We've sung it a thousand times to our children, but have you ever really listened to the words … kind of a morbid rhyme don't you think? I was actually reading nursery rhymes to my twins the other day and my boys asked what this one meant. Maybe I have stock market on the brain, but I felt it was a very a fitting metaphor for how naïve the average investor is.

Think about it … when the bough breaks YOUR cradle will fall. The tree is the stock market and what will happen to the bulk of Americans (the "babies") and their nest eggs (the "cradle and all") when we have another financial crisis like we had in the early 2000s and again in 2008??

I am continually amazed at how in life there are a small handful of experiences that define our future, three to five experiences that influence you in such a grand way that they guide you toward a future direction. Given how much of our life is on auto-pilot I find it quite impressive how just a few moments in time can shape our entire future.

These experiences can be good ones that we want to replicate, OR for me I've found the bad experiences are the most impactful. As an example, one of my first corporate jobs right out of college was working for someone that just didn't have a clue on how to service his customers, and by watching the frustration of his customers I vowed to treat my customers with the highest level of respect and service … to treat them more like partners than customers. Three businesses later that one experience has completely shaped my business life and how I interact with people … it had a huge impact on me.

One of my earliest experiences with Wall Street had such an enormous impact on me that it really defined my future in the financial world, first as an investor and eventually as our main focus at Resnn Investments. It occurred 25 years ago but is such a vivid memory that it feels like it occurred only yesterday. I was 17 years old and although I didn't feel like a kid when this occurred I look back now and realize how naïve and young I really was. I remember the day well, it was October 1987 and the entire experience lasted no more than a few minutes over dinner with my mom and dad.

You may or may not remember this time in the stock market but for me this was a defining moment for my future. It was Monday, October 19th and the market had a bad down day. The previous week the stock market lost over 7% and the week before it lost 3% … but today alone the market closed down 11%! Imagine how you would feel if I took 20% of your entire net worth and flushed it down the toilet over a 2 week period of time.

As a 17-year-old I obviously didn't really care about anything outside of my little selfish world. Economics was a class I was taking but as a typical teenager … if it didn't directly affect me I was pretty oblivious. Yet this time, this evening had a dramatic impact on me.

Dinner started normally with my mom cooking, my dad coming home from work, and small talk occurring. I used to do homework at the kitchen table before dinner so it was normal for me to hear the small talk between my parents. They started talking about what happened in the market that day and suddenly I noticed my dad having trouble forming sentences. He was really shaken up and fighting back tears. I obviously started listening much more intently as the talk went to their 401k and investment accounts and what potential impact this would have on their future.

What was so strong about that moment was to see the fear in my dad. I was lucky enough to have a good upbringing. My parents loved me and worked hard for my well being to which I am incredibly grateful, especially now that I am a parent of three boys myself and know the selfless sacrifice you give unconditionally every day to them.

My parents were a rock to me, they defined stability at a time when stability was sooo important for a teenager trying to find his way in the world, but yet … here was a rare glimpse into my dad and his vulnerability. I've only seen my dad afraid three times in my life, and 2 of those times had dramatic effect on me. I remember feeling so many emotions that evening. I wanted to help them, to fix it for them. I wanted to tell them everything would be fine. I wished I hadn't been home to hear their conversation, mostly … I just wanted to go back to the way it was just minutes before.

To watch my dad look so helpless and afraid of his future, of our future, is something I hope not many people have to endure in their own life.

Although I was still too young to really understand the world and how financial markets worked, I remember thinking there must be a better way. I can only imagine what my dad went through for the next year and how he came to terms with the loss, but suffice to say I knew that I never wanted to experience what he went through on that day and more importantly I NEVER want my kids to see fear from their 'rock.'

Flashing forward to today, I am happy that I can now say with 100% confidence that I will never experience the feeling of helplessness that my dad must have felt that evening, and my hope in writing this book is that I can pass that same safety on to you and your children. You see this isn't about percentage gains or losses; we are talking about things that are so much greater than profit and loss. We are talking about the difference between happiness and not, about providing for loved ones and being as 'solid as a rock' to the ones you care about.

Chapter 3

My Short Retirement

IN **2008 … I RETIRED.** I was 38 years old. Not bad ... if I do say so myself.

My wife had stopped working when N (my oldest) was a wee one (roughly 8 years before), she didn't need to. The story is a little more complex than this, but for all intents and purposes I checked out of the corporate world and focused on my most important asset … my family.

But first, I need to rewind about a year prior to give you the full picture. Our son (he was our only at the time) was nine and we felt that he was finally old enough to be able to send him to Grandma's for two weeks so my wife and I could take an extended vacation. We decided to take an Alaskan Cruise for ten days and afterward drive through the Canadian Rockies for another week. You have to understand that this trip was a VERY big deal. It was our first real *adult* trip since our boy was born and the first time that we actually focused on what we wanted vs. always catering to his needs and wants.

You can imagine how apprehensive my wife was about going, yet after a few days she fell into the new routine and really enjoyed herself without worrying too much about our son who was being safely taken care of by my mom.

Long story short we had an AMAZING time with each other. We really found each other again and came back so much closer. If you're married with children you understand what I am talking about. Years of putting your children first, your work a close second, your spouse (and yourself) last really takes a toll on your marriage and unfortunately for many … it destroys it.

I have many older clients that unfortunately got lost along the way; once the kids were grown up and out of the house they looked across the table at their spouse and only saw a stranger.

They had grown apart over the years. While shuffling their kids from this practice to that practice, helping with homework and at the end of the day being so exhausted, they forgot to give their spouse that little extra that is so important. It's ironic that the very thing that should pull you closer, your children, ultimately does the opposite. All the love and energy that used to go toward your spouse now is channeled toward your children and if you are not careful over time this can cause irreparable damage. It takes work, and a lot of it to keep that fire alive between the two of you.

We struggled with the same issues and I was particularly guilty. Work and my kiddo got the priority and my wife got whatever was left over. I remember justifying it in my head that the client that needed me at 10 at night was an emergency and that my wife would understand *this time*. But *this time* eventually became *every time* as it became a regular occurrence that I was not around for her. Fortunately I'm happy to say now (after 20 years of marriage) that we definitely have things figured out and she is now my priority right next to my children.

Needless to say this trip was an important experience for both of us. It helped us to remember why we fell in love with each other in the first place and why it was important to stay focused on making each other the priority. We came back so excited for the future. We got a glimpse of 'adult life' again as we experienced the simple things that all of us take for granted sans children … sleeping in, being able to keep driving even though it is dinner time, going out late at night without worrying about having to be 'on your game' early the next morning. Even though our boy was only 9, for the first time ever, we saw 'the light at the end of the tunnel.' We came back rejuvenated and ready to conquer the next number of years knowing we had so much to look forward to after we successfully got him off to college.

You see when he was about 4 years old we decided that maybe we weren't cut out for raising children. I won't get into the specifics here but we had a really difficult time when he was a young buck and ultimately decided that maybe him being an only child was the best for our family.

Life has a funny way of *nicely* changing your direction doesn't it? Of course , you know what I'm going to say next. Just when you think you are in charge of your future … whammo!

I think the best I've ever heard it described was from the movie *Father of the Bride, Part 2* with Steve Martin. If you haven't seen Father of the Bride (the first or second or even the originals from the 1950's), I highly recommend all of them … good fun! The second movie starts out with George Banks (played by Steve Martin) talking about his experience over the past year, accepting the fact that his daughter is now married and not around anymore …

> *George Banks: "Father of the bride. I never thought I'd say this but that whole experience was a piece of cake compared to the roller coaster I've been on this past year.*
>
> *I admit it took me a while to recover from the wedding, but eventually life got back to normal, which is exactly the way I prefer life to be. After the dust settled, I began to realize what a lucky guy I was. I had a wonderful home filled with memories and completely paid for; a wife I love just as much as the day I married her; a daughter, independent, self-sufficient, married, working, happy; a son blossoming in the middle of middle school; and a son-in-law, gainfully employed and very often out of town on business.*
>
> *Life was sweet. I felt for the first time ahead of the game.*
>
> *Then it dawned on me...I was a mere 5 years away from freedom. Soon I'd be a father with one kid married and the other off in college, and that started me thinking...what was I gonna do with all*

> *that free time? Anything I wanted! Maybe I'd take up fly fishing, travel to exotic places, climb Mount Everest.*
>
> *I was feeling on top of the world.*
>
> *And that's when they lowered the boom on me. It was like that old joke, 'All those who think they have it made take one step forward...not so fast George Banks!' It was about a year ago when it all started...well, nine months ago to be exact..."*

Yep … that trip that I mentioned earlier … well I can tell you that that was the last one my wife and I will be enjoying … for a long time. Let's just say that roughly 9 months after that cruise … our lives were forever changed …

I remember the day I found out like it was yesterday. I was my son's soccer coach and it was late in the day, we were on the field doing drills with the kids when I got a call from my beautiful wife. She sounded different, and wanted to come by the field to *show me something*. I couldn't understand why it couldn't wait until I got home, but I agreed and she came down. When she arrived, I sent the boys out for laps so I could talk to her.

Walking over to her, I saw she had something in her hand but I couldn't make it out. When I got in front of her not a word was said … she immediately handed me a black box. It was an ornate jewelry box (the kind that holds a necklace) that I had given to her the Christmas prior. I couldn't imagine why she was giving me jewelry and why it couldn't wait until I got home. I immediately panicked thinking I had missed our anniversary yet after doing some quick math I knew I wasn't in hot water *this time*. Phew … I dodged that bullet … or so I thought.

When I opened the jewelry box, there was a long stick with a plus sign in the middle of it. Pretty funny … she put the 'pregnancy stick' inside the jewelry box to show me that she was pregnant.

There was a very interesting study done a few years ago on the effects of your brain during traumatic or life threatening moments and how your brain seems to have the ability to slow down time. In actuality it doesn't slow time, but as a survival mechanism your focus sharpens so much as you take in everything around you that it gives the illusion of slow motion since you are absorbing all the details like the color of the grass, the wind rustling the leaves; noises and smells that you normally don't pay attention to suddenly become part of the memory.

At that moment in time, on the soccer field, as my brain was trying to comprehend what I was looking at, what changes it meant for me, for us … well let's just say this was one of the longest moments I have ever experienced. Needless to say, soccer practice was cancelled that night.

We went home that night and stayed up most of the night talking. The decision was made for her to go to the doctor's office the next day to have them confirm, "just in case" the test was not correct.

Chapter 4

An 'Ordinary' Doctor's Visit

The doctor not only confirmed, but he wanted to have a high-end ultrasound done because he said based on the tests he thought Elizabeth was much further along than she had thought. So the next day we went together to the ultrasound excited to see our new baby for the first time.

What started out as an fun trip to 'meet' our baby turned out to be, well … let's just say this was the second moment in my life where my brain 'slowed time.'

The ultrasound started very normal by getting to see our little baby and hearing his heart beat. The room was full of excitement. The doctor confirmed that Elizabeth was only a few weeks along, even though the previous tests showed otherwise. Then the doctor said that there was only one baby in there … to which I ignorantly replied, **"Oh, thank God … if there were two, I think I would have killed myself."**

It was at that moment where I should have been desperately searching for some wood to knock on, but having failed to do so, the next words out of the doctor's mouth was … "oh wait a minute, I spoke too soon. Do you see there? … and also there … you're going to have two babies!!"

They say when you die that your life flashes before your eyes, that all the most amazing events quickly flip by like an animation flip book … I am certain this moment will be in my 'book' when I kick the bucket. Pay attention, because this is the moment that I will have on my death bed … I'm reminded of the movie *A Christmas Story* (another wonderfully funny movie I highly recommend) ... **"FUDGGGGGGGEEEEEEE."** You see my wife shouted out the word above, "Only she didn't say 'Fudge.' She said THE word, the big one, the queen-mother of dirty words, the 'F-dash-dash-dash' word!"

Looking back at that moment, it was quite hilarious. The young naïve nurse in the room was sooo excited for us UNTIL she saw my wife's reaction, the doctor had no idea how to handle the situation, I was a blithering idiot hyperventilating in the corner, while my wife went from a beautifully, glowing 'Glinda - the Good Witch' to a green 'Wicked Witch of the West' within 2.5 seconds.

I don't really remember the car ride home that day, but it's safe to say that time really does heal wounds because once we got over the initial jolt … within a few weeks both Elizabeth and I became VERY excited and started planning for our inevitable doom … cough cough … I mean arrivals.

Chapter 5

Multiplication

Needless to say, things fell back into routine after a few weeks and we started planning for the next phase in our life. As we started pondering our fate, we were struck by questions like how do you feed two babies at the same time, how do you calm two crying babies at the same time and the inevitable … how do you sleep when two babies are waking up every one to two hours (independent of each other, I might add) to be fed.

Retirement … this is where it all came into play. Looking at what we had in front of us, the logical answer came to me that I needed (and wanted) to be around for the first few years of my twin'kies life. Realistically we needed 2 people around to be able to care for these little ones and who better than my wife and I. I remember approaching my wife with the idea and at first she thought it was preposterous, but after going over our situation, we both realized it was totally doable.

You see, I consider myself quite successful. In fact, I would go so far as to say I'm living the American Dream, complete with 2.3 children :) … well, really one 15-year-old and twin 5 year olds. I am 43 years old, live in a 6,500 square foot house with one of the best views of the Colorado Rockies and Downtown Denver combined, I work from my home and drive a very nice Mercedes. I have a vacation home in the ski town of Steamboat Springs Colorado; take literally the entire month of July off every year to spend time with my family. Best of all, I moved 3 years ago to Colorado (from Los Angeles) not because of a job relocation, but because my wife and I wanted a better life for our children … in fact, money had literally nothing to do with our decision.

In all intents and purposes, from the outside I have a dream life, and from the inside it is even better. Because the pressure of money and wealth gathering has been removed I am able to focus on enjoying my time and the people that I love. I love my life, and quite honestly wouldn't change a thing about it.

Oh, and I forgot to mention, I am completely self-made. I started with not a single dime to my name and built what I have from hard work.

Ok … so now that we've established that I'm an arrogant, pompous dick … well, not so fast. In fact, this is really the first time I have ever documented the wealth that I have generated using the approaches contained in this book. If you knew me, you would be surprised by the past paragraphs, because money and specifically the 'art' of showing it off is something that I've never felt was a need or important to do. Spending money just because you have it never made sense to me. Watching the celebrities that I worked so closely with that were literally making $10 million for 6 months of work spend and spend and spend and never seem to achieve happiness in their lives had a big impact on me in this regard. I used to joke with my wife that in Hollywood you weren't trying to keep up with the Jones, but rather the Spielberg's … and we all know what a futile effort that would be.

"The root of all evil is not money; it's the lack of money that is the root of all evil." – *Mark Twain*

I remember being in Las Vegas when I was 20-ish years old playing Craps. That particular evening, the table was hot and there was a crowd around the table as the winnings were adding up. People were hootin' and hollering after each roll of the dice and the energy was so intense you could feel it. Suddenly a nondescript guy squeezed his way through the crowd and took a place across from me at the table. He was wearing sweats.

He stood out to me, because as you know in Las Vegas people generally get dressed up to gamble particularly in the higher end casinos. I was standing next to men in sports coats and woman in dresses and in he comes looking quite comfortable in his beat up sweats. Anyway, he motioned the pit boss who then whispered something to the dealer at our table, and suddenly another employee of the casino comes running up with a double decker tray of chips which he handed to Mr. Sweats. The chips were a color I had never seen before and as this happened a hush came over the table. It turns out, they were $10,000.00 chips and over the next 30 minutes he proceeded to drop more money than I think I had ever seen up to that point in my life. At any given time he would have between $30,000 and $60,000 on the table and periodically he would lose it. What's more amazing is how loose he was with the chips tipping the dealers and waitress, once he even dropped a few chips on the floor and although he did pick them up … he didn't seem to be too concerned about losing these.

Long story short, I learned a lot that evening about the value of money. I saw the worst dressed guy in the casino with more money in his hand than most will make in their entire life. I realized that it doesn't take flashy suits, watches, cars, etc to be comfortable with yourself. In fact, after witnessing this event, I continued watching how people use money and what I generally found was that the people with the sharpest clothes or fanciest cars were usually the people that didn't have a lot of extra, whereas the people that tried to blend in were the ones with substantial wealth.

For me, I look at money and more specifically wealth as having one and only one purpose, the ability to create freedom.

In fact, having *freedom* and therefore *choices* is the only reason why wealth is important to me. Money gives me the freedom to spend the morning in my kid's kindergarten class, the freedom to take a day off and go skiing with friends, the freedom to take a month off every July to spend time with my family, the freedom to say no to a problem client (more on this in my upcoming book entitled *Consultant to the Stars*), and the freedom to take the first 4 years of my twins lives out of the corporate world … retired.

In fact, my company name, Resnn Investments, LLC is an acronym for my immediate family. I felt it fitting to name the company RESNN; after all ... these are the people that my goals are shaped around. You see, for me wealth is not about driving a Ferrari or using private jets to get from destination A to B, but it is ultimately about providing for loved ones, spending the future with the people you care about and having enough to fulfill whatever emotional goals you have.

Now with all the above said, I will say that I work harder than most people by far, but I do it by choice. Besides my family, I am not tied to any one or ever forced to do something I don't want to. I live life by MY choices, MY decisions and that is what wealth has given me.

I merely state the above, not to brag, but to tell you that what I have discovered and share in this book is very real. It works, and quite frankly I'm not only the president but I'm a customer too. I believe so much in the techniques introduced here that I couldn't fathom investing any other way EVER. It is the path to phenomenal wealth, but more importantly as I will share with you the path to a stress free life.

Chapter 6

Big Data

As I mentioned earlier, I spent the years around the millennium building up two companies in the technology / software industry. The first company worked exclusively with high profile celebrities helping them with their technology needs. We did everything from recovering data off of a laptop that was thrown out of a 9th story hotel window (broken glass and all) after one of our celeb clients threw a tantrum, building movie editing stations at their Malibu beach houses and then teaching them how to edit their own big screen movies digitally, renting military satellites in order to stay connected to the outside world while filming on location in Antarctica, running encrypted video uplinks before Skype and certainly before iPad's and FaceTime existed, creating enormous security communication systems to keep retired military and secret service agents in the loop while protecting celebrities in other countries, and yes … we even did the occasional "I can't print," or "how do you send an email" service calls.

Working exclusively with Hollywood's elite provided me with an amazing understanding of how 'the other half' live and more importantly how they create, maintain and sometimes lose all their wealth. There are a handful of specific traits that differentiate the *haves* from the *have-nots* … the affluent from others. Working side by side with celebrities for over 15 years helped me to clearly identify these specific differences. In fact, my upcoming book, *Consultant to the Stars* goes into great detail on this topic if you have an interest in learning more, but one huge differentiator between the Super Affluent and *the rest of us* is that they understand the power of getting their money, time and resources to work for them.

At my previous business, Greater Than Data, we billed for man hours and for us our typical programmer could bill 25 – 30 hours a week (the rest of the time was spent training, in meetings and administrative overhead), so I know I could only earn as much money as time in the day. As a result, **I realized early on that my business could make me good money, but it was what I did with that money that was going to make me wealthy. I could spend it, or use it to make more ...** ***to put it to work.***

As I mentioned previously, I had taken a hands-off approach to my investments after my 'Ferrari Dreams' incident and was focusing on the day-to-day operations of my business when one day I had an epiphany moment. I remember the exact day; it was a Saturday in late February 2004. It was tax time and I was getting my financial statements together to go to my accountant the following week.

I was looking over my investments and specifically a 401k statement when I suddenly realized that I hadn't made a dime in about 10 years! I remember feeling sick to my stomach as I walked to the garage to dig out some old financial statements to verify my findings. This couldn't be ... not one dime in 10 years??? Come on, we had just been through one of the greatest tech booms in the history of mankind, and I didn't profit from it??

You can imagine how frustrated I was that morning and maybe a better adjective is that I was quite honestly angry at what I discovered. What were the financial advisors that I had been paying all those years doing? What did their fees do for me? It was at that exact moment that Resnn was born. I still had no idea that I would eventually go into business in the financial industry, but what I did know was that I could do better. My day ultimately was wasted in terms of preparing for the accountant visit but ended up being the most profitable moment of my life.

I'm always amazed when this happens to me, one discovery leads me down a new path in life; something that is so cloudy one day becomes crystal clear the next. When those moments happen I'm always amazed at how I had not 'seen the light' before, how it took a specific experience to open my mind up to embrace a new reality. Yet I suppose this isn't all that odd after all. If you think about it, most *inventions* or ideas are created this way, out of frustration from the status quo. A feeling of discomfort causes us to search for a better way. Obviously, if on that February morning I looked at my 401k statement and was pleased with the performance over the past 10 years, I wouldn't have given it a second thought and life would have continued as is.

> ***"Restlessness is discontent and discontent is the first necessity of progress"*** – *Thomas A. Edison*

Can you think of a life altering discovery that changed your outlook and future as a result?

I spent most of the weekend pondering my next steps and what programs I could create to further this endeavor. You see, I realized that what my second firm did for our customers' was really not much different from what was needed for my investments.

At Greater Than Data, we took a quantitative data-centric approach to solving various client problems. We would take millions and millions of lines of data and try to find some recognizable pattern in them to help companies find more efficient ways of doing things, or to find missing revenue streams, etc. We really didn't know it at the time, how ahead of the technology world we were. This was before the days of Google Analytics or any form of *Information Management* firms. In fact, we were forerunners of what is now called 'Big Data.'

At that time, I really couldn't imagine working in any other capacity. I really enjoyed the work and was continually fascinated at how powerful the analysis of data could be; how organizing data in certain ways would reveal little hidden treasures.

If you haven't figured it out already, I was AND STILL AM a complete Geek. Next to my wife, data is my second true love. I remember one particular evening coming home from work and telling her about a pattern that we discovered that helped save one of our customers a few million dollars (literally). It was that day that I knew I needed to focus on this as a career and this was when Greater Than Data was born.

So moving our data analysis techniques away from solving our customer's problems, into finding a better way to protect and invest assets in the stock market was a natural next step for me. I must say, initially I was very giddy … my Ferrari Dreams started creeping back into my head, but I quickly became humbled. You see, the effort was much harder than I thought. The original goal was to find consistent and reliable patterns in the market that could be profited from. What I assumed would take a week to figure out ended up becoming a multimillion dollar 3 year research project at Greater Than Data. My programmers didn't really know what they were working on, except that it had something to do with analyzing the stock market.

The journey was long and frustrating, but being that we were working with data, I was having a good time nonetheless. I spent my days watching the market and evenings reading as much as I could, coming up with new theories to test in future revisions. This is the period of time I mentioned previously where I went down A LOT of rabbit holes, spending literally thousands of wasted hours testing bogus claims from various books and investment *gurus*.

> ***"Don't let the fear of striking out hold you back"***
> *- Babe Ruth*

Yet, many of these *wasted* journeys would end up at a door that when opened would lead me a little further down the road. They each contributed to my knowledge and further theories that ultimately led to the success of the project.

> ***"Do not be embarrassed by your failures, learn from them and start again."*** *– Richard Branson*

As an example, our first endeavor was to gather as much historical data as we could on the market. You understand that we were using complex statistical analysis and the more data that we had at our fingertips the more accurate our analysis would be. Ultimately we were able to gather almost 100 years of market data, minute by minute, every single transaction of every company in the US stock exchanges for all history. Literally millions and millions of lines of data, and as we started analyzing this data one thing became very clear … corrections (declines) happen and they happen on a regular and consistent basis.

In fact, looking over history we found that corrections happen on average between 2 and 3 times every single year and when they do we generally get a 5-10% decline. But, every 2-3 years we have a much larger decline usually between 20 to 30% (2008, 2010 and 2011 are great examples of this), and as we've seen over the past decade, we clearly go through periods of much stronger declines.

This correction *discovery* started me on a very different path than my original mission. What began as a way to find the *next big winner* in the stock market quickly morphed into a defensive approach. Imagine how much easier it would be to beat the average investor when the market was acting well, if I was able to avoid the next 20% decline. Heck … doing the math … avoiding a 20% drop in my net worth meant that I could miss the next 25% rise in value and still be the same as everyone else.

This might already be obvious to you, but if you quickly work the numbers you will see something interesting. Did you know that a 50% drop in your net worth requires a 100% rise to just get back to break-even?

Think about it … if you have $100.00 and lose half of it (50%), the value becomes $50.00. Now what do you have to make in order to get back to $100.00? You have to double your money; you have to make 100% on your original $50.00 investment in order to recoup the 50% loss. Kind of crazy.

Most people think that if you lose 50%, you just have to earn 50% to break-even … not so.

The math gets kind of crazy as we go further along … a 60% loss requires a 150% gain, 80% loss requires a 400% gain and a 90% loss (as what happened between 1999 and 2003 in the Nasdaq) requires a 900% gain just to get back to break-even!

The other issue that I discovered was related to time. If an investor endures a 50% loss, how much time is wasted while they just try to get their portfolio back to break-even? Remember I mentioned in the beginning of this book, that the dot-com crash has yet to break-even … 13 years later. What opportunity cost do you lose while you are waiting for your money just to get back to break-even? If you are like most investors you don't have 13+ years to waste.

The majority of investors in the market are between 50 and 65 years old, which happen to be the most critical time for wealth accumulation. This age bracket is considered the most pivotal set of years that separate the super affluent and the upper middle class during their retirement years. The reason for this is that most people are at the top of their earnings potential at this age, so their income is high. They also are at the point where their children are leaving the house which dramatically reduces their expenses and allows them to focus on saving more. With lower expenses and higher income, these years are a pivotal time to separate your net worth from everyone else out there.

With this said, there is no age where one can *afford* to wait for breakeven. You need your money when you need it … and I'm sure I'm not the first to tell you that your financial goals don't always work out as planned. Sometimes the unexpected happens. People tend to use bad news; "saving for a rainy day" like getting diagnosed with cancer as an example of needing money ahead of schedule, but there are good moments as well …

I mentioned the story about my twins earlier. Put yourself in my shoes and think about how I felt the day I found out. I went from feeling pretty darn good about my financial situation; I was running a successful business that had very low overhead and a very reliable clientele, I drove a Porsche, my wife drove a Range

Rover, we lived in a multi-million dollar home in the Los Angeles hills and my only son went to a private elementary school that cost more than most colleges in annual tuition. Then in an instant, my household went from three to five … almost doubling over night. You can imagine how poor I felt that day. How was I going to be able to afford three private schools, car seats, food for all of us, etc. … the numbers were boggling!

As you probably have heard, it is a good idea to have 3-6 months of living expenses sitting in a liquid account such as an FDIC insured bank savings account. You will basically earn nothing on this savings, but that is not the point of it. You should have money invested, designed to grow your net worth, and money set aside as a safety net and the 3-6 month expense account is for safety. The two investments serve different purposes. The safety net is there for the what-if scenario … you get hurt, lose your job, etc. If you are self-employed I would suggest that you save closer to 6 months, vs. if you are employed by a large firm that has excellent benefits, 3 months is probably sufficient. But always have at least 3 … as I write this, we are in the middle of the US Government in a shut down with hundreds of thousands of government employees being furloughed. Heck … if you can't count on a paycheck from the US Government who can you count on??

Notice I suggested 3-6 months *living expenses* and not 3-6 months of income. As I've said previously, it really doesn't matter how much you make, it only matters how much you keep and this applies here as well. I have many celebrity clients that make literally 6 figures a month (I have a few that make 6 figures a week!!) yet their expenses are much lower. At the end of the day if something *bad* happens, you only need to cover your bills and nothing more obviously.

This account is only designed for a short-term emergency; to give you time to come up with a

contingency plan if whatever *bad news* looks like it is going to become a longer-term problem.

At 38 years old … I suddenly needed to make certain that my money was there for me and time was not on my side. This was not a short-term *emergency* where my 3-6 month savings account could help. I needed a long-term solution. Waiting for 5-10 years for my investment just to get back to break-even was no longer an option. I'll be honest … I don't think anyone should be held captive by their investments.

Defensive Thinking or what I have coined 'Protective Investment Management' is ironically how the professional *Institutional Investors* approach investing. I will delve into this a bit later, but in the mean time I want to encourage you to start looking at the stock market from a different perspective. Instead of trying to find the next big winner, try to look at your individual investments in a more defensive way. The questions we want to tackle are not: "what is the next Google or Apple?" but rather, "Is the market a healthy place to invest right now?" "How much am I willing to lose in order to gain xx" and lastly, "how much time can I afford to lose if my investments go terribly wrong?"

Chapter 7

'Buy and Hold,' a Risky Venture

"Do you have any idea how cheap stocks are now? Wall Street is now being called Wal-Mart Street." *- Jay Leno.*

Seeing how regular the stock market declines, how intense the drops are and most importantly how long it can take just to get back to break-even, I started wondering if a 'buy and hold' approach made sense anymore.

The greatest thing about 'buy and hold' is that it is easy to do. It takes very little time. I remember running my first business and listening to the nightly news on the drive home, hearing how the DOW was up (or down) and that was pretty much all I wanted to know related to my investments. So, although I feel there is a substantially better way to invest I do understand why most people choose to use a 'buy and hold' approach. In fact as a Financial Advisor, I love the concept of a 'buy and hold' strategy because very few people have the leisure or desire to spend time managing their investments.

Yet, the simplicity of 'buy and hold' is also its' greatest flaw; since no one is watching your investments, you are completely at the whim of the market, and herein lies the fundamental problem with a 'buy and hold' approach, there is no built-in safety mechanism to protect you from decline.

I don't have to pound this concept in; if you already invest in the market I'm certain you have felt the pain of massive loss in the recent past. But, it is important to understand that if you choose to rely on a 'buy and hold' approach, you have to be prepared to weather a large decline.

So, the next natural question becomes … if I still want to stick with a 'buy and hold' approach, how can I minimize the negative impact? Most Financial Advisors would give you two suggestions … Dollar Cost Averaging (DCA) and Diversification. I intend to show you how both are bad advice.

Let's start with Dollar Cost Averaging. For those of you who do not know what DCA is, basically the idea is that you consistently invest in the market in small amounts on a regular basis. As an example, every week you invest $100.00 for the next 10 years (52k total), instead of investing $52,000.00 all at once. You *average* your cost by buying as the market gains and losses as a result you never run the risk of buying at the absolute high or the absolute low … you are average.

Similar to 'buy and hold', Dollar Cost Averaging requires little to no time commitment which is the real benefit to DCA. You make a decision to setup the account and forget about it as each month a small amount gets invested. It couldn't be easier. Which leads to the second benefit, it requires no discipline. Most people that have come to me because they didn't start investing early enough in their life and are now desperately trying to *catch up*, blame lack of discipline as the main culprit. They tell me they didn't have the discipline when they found their bank account had an extra 1k in it. Instead of investing it in the market, they would find something to buy. Again, with our busy lives I totally understand how this happens and having an automatic sweep from your checking account into an investment account alleviates this problem. Over time this can really add up to a huge amount of money. To use the example above would you miss $50.00 or $100.00 a week? If not … then you can see that over 10 years it really adds up, and although you certainly can't retire off of $52,000.00, it gets you going in the right direction.

Now, let's discuss the drawbacks of Dollar Cost Averaging. You probably already see the first problem with DCA; the goal is *average performance* which seems like an odd goal given the risk you are taking by being in the stock market.

Ironically, when you look at studies of the performance using dollar-cost averaging, it doesn't compare favorably with the strategy of investing a lump sum and letting it ride, defeating the entire purpose of DCA in the first place. The simple reason is that stocks generally trend upward over time. Given that, from a profitability point of view you're generally better off investing the largest amount you can as soon as you can rather than dribbling the money into the market slowly over a period of months and years.

With that said, I'm not so concerned about this since there is a much bigger issue. The biggest issue with Dollar Cost Averaging is that (similar to 'buy and hold') it offers no protection for your account. If the market starts falling, although it is good that you are buying at lower and lower prices … there is no guarantee that the market will stop falling. So, although you are buying the same stock for a cheaper price, it really doesn't matter if the market continues to fall lower.

"Losers average losers." *– Paul Tudor Jones*

There's a saying in the stock market, "Never catch a falling knife." It basically means just because an investment is cheaper today than yesterday doesn't make it a good deal, because you simply don't know if tomorrow will bring even lower prices. Looking at 2000 through 2002 we saw a great example of this. In 2000, the NASDAQ lost 39.3%, 2001 another 21.1% and finally in 2002 it fell again 31.5%. If you were buying every week for those three years you lost, lost and lost some more.

So, although Dollar Cost Averaging provides simplicity it does so at a price, it doesn't provide what I (and the Pros) feel is the most important factor to consider in any investment strategy, risk control and safety mechanisms.

Chapter 8

Diversification

"Broad diversification is plainly and simply a hedge for ignorance" - *William O'Neil*

Diversification was one of the most interesting findings in my 100 year analysis of the market. We have all been trained from day one to "don't put all your eggs in one basket." In fact, I would say this is the number 1 *rule* that all financial advisors, mutual fund companies and brokerage firms preach, and yet, the logic is flawed because it is based on out-of-date studies.

I hate to use such strong words, but we've all been *brainwashed* to put 30% into international markets to help reduce the impact in the event of a US market decline, yet if you look over the past 20 – 30 years … this type of diversification simply doesn't work anymore. The world's markets are no longer separate *islands*, they move very closely in step with each other, particularly when declining. Poor economic reports in one major market like the United States will upset the entire world's economic position, and over the last few decades the performance of these various world markets shows exactly this.

Take a look at the '2008 Performance by Market' chart below showing all world's indexes in 2008 and you can see that there was literally NO safe place to put your money. Regardless of where you invested in the world, you lost between 30 and 70%.

2008 Performance by Market

Dow Jones Industrial Index	-39.4%	MSCI World Index	-43.1%
S&P 500 Composite Index	-41.9%	MSCI Emerging Markets Ind	-53.8%
Nasdaq Composite Index	-42.5%		
Russell 2000 Index	-41.7%	German DAX Index	-40.5%
Toronto 300 Comp Index	-36.3%	Paris CAC 40 Index	-43.6%
		UK FTSE 100 Index	-44.6%
Australian All Ordinaries Index	-42.5%	Vienna ATX Index	-56.6%
NZ Wellington NZSX 50 Index	-33.0%	Brussels 20 Index	-52.9%
Nikkei 225 Index	-54.7%	Copenhagen KFX Index	-42.2%
Singapore STRAITS Times Index	-49.3%	Helsinki Index	-52.2%
		Dublin ISEQ Index	-69.5%
Hang Seng Index	-53.2%	Amsterdam AEX Index	-49.8%
Shanghai Comp Index	-67.1%	Oslo Benchmark Index	-50.5%
Bombay Sensex Index	-55.7%	Lisbon PSI 20 Index	-51.3%
Brazilian Bovespa Index	-63.5%	Spanish IBEX 35 Index	-37.9%
Russian Trading System Index	-65.4%	Swiss SPI General Index	-37.5%
Venezuela Carcas Index	-29.7%	Stockholm General Index	-51.2%
South Africa FTSE/JSE All Share Inde	-36.1%		

Diversification clearly used to work. Before 1980 the US markets did not correlate with the movement of any major world index, yet since 1980, every year that passes, all of the world markets have steadily moved closer and closer in step with one another.

As I mentioned above, this was quite a shocking discovery for me, although after thinking about it … it kind of makes sense. In the last 30 years, globalization is probably the largest change that has occurred in our business worlds. Most (if not all) publicly traded companies have customers AND employees all over the world. The global effects of a U.S. only recession are massive.

Imagine the impact of one company like Apple or Google if their sales were down 20% for the year … what would occur? Well, first there would be layoffs and not just in America, but their workforce is all over the world. They also hire thousands of small businesses as consultants that would get axed which would result in these companies letting go of key personnel as well. My first company alone hired hundreds of programmers across the world as independent contractors, if our customers had no work for us; these programmers also had no work.

The same is true with diversifying across different sectors. Most financial advisors will suggest you invest across a broad spectrum of US based sectors (manufacturing, banking, technology), but the same issue is present, there is no safety in this type of investing.

Three out of four stocks move in the same direction as the market, so if the market is going up, you have a 75% chance that the company or sector you are invested in will move up with it, and if the market is going down … you have a 25% chance (one in four) that the stock or sector you are invested in will buck the trend and ignore the market's decline.

> ***"A rising tide will lift all boats"*** *- John F Kennedy*

Here's the interesting thing though, diversification does work in the opposite direction, in up years. If you are looking to maximize gains … putting your money to work in different global markets will give you some outsized performance numbers. While the S&P500 may have a sluggish year and only return 3%, Japan's Nikkei may return over 30%, or with stocks … maybe the banking sector has a stellar year while technology is lackluster. But remember, you don't know ahead of time which market will outperform, and when the market starts to decline (and it will), three out of four stocks will fall with it, period.

Bottom line, diversification can increase your returns in good years, but it does not necessarily provide safety. As I mentioned above, this came as a huge shock for me. I always assumed by putting my money in three or four different locations, it was safer, but history clearly shows … it isn't. Just because 30% of your money is in an international mutual fund doesn't mean it won't drop right alongside the US market when we have the next 30% correction, and for me and my client investments, safety is my number one priority. Making sure your money is safe from massive decline is the easiest way to make certain your money will be there for you when you need it.

The important thing to understand here is that investing techniques like Dollar Cost Averaging and Diversification aren't by themselves inherently evil … you just need to understand what they provide and don't provide for you. Protection is NOT something that 'buy and hold', diversification and DCA give you. This might be ok for you, it's obviously your decision, but don't be naïve into thinking you are safe by investing this way

Chapter 9

Passive Investing vs. Active Investing

When looking at investing styles, there are generally two schools of thought, Passive Investing and Active Investing. Passive Investing is basically 'buy and hold.' Passive Investors will tell you that there really is no way to time the market because that would involve knowing what the future will bring or knowing something that no one else knows (i.e. insider trading) and therefore since that is impossible, you might as well not even try to beat the market but rather just invest and ride the ups and downs as they come. Passive investors will say things like "if you missed just the 10 best days of the market over the past 20 years, your return would be significantly lower than a 'buy and hold.'"

You already know my gripes with a 'buy and hold' technique in that it offers no protection of your assets whatsoever, but in some ways I agree with the passive investment argument since there really is no way to know what the future brings. To use a very real example ... what if tomorrow a bomb went off at the White House? The market would obviously react negatively and unless you were somehow connected with the crime, you obviously could not have predicted that this would have occurred and therefore you would have been at the mercy of the market as a result.

> ***"As a speculator you must embrace disorder and chaos."*** *– Louis Bacon*

Active investors, on the other hand, feel they can do better than a 'buy and hold' by picking opportune moments or opportune positions. They believe there are specific situations that can move the odds in their favor and their reasoning is usually quite varied from seasonal cycles (stocks generally do better in November, December and January than every other month of the year) to fundamentals (low PE or PEG ratios, low margins), to beliefs in certain technologies or sectors (3D printing, solar technologies, etc). Generally speaking, they use some form of historical analysis to conclude their findings. As an example, Warren Buffett looks for companies that are greatly unvalued and unpopular and buys them at opportune moments and holds them for many years. His analysis of out of favor companies and their ability to turnaround the company has led him to be one of the greatest investors of all time.

Active investors know that they are still at the whim of the market, they obviously can't stop that White House bombing but the goal is to move the odds in their favor. If a bomb goes off tomorrow, I don't care what stock that active investor was in, he is going to lose money in the short-term, but if the bomb does not go off the idea behind active investing is that he is putting himself in a position that has a favorable risk/reward ratio that over time will pay off on a consistent basis.

The debate as to whether passive or active investing is better is heated and one that has been going on for many years, and will continue to go on for many more. There are periods of time when one style will outperform the other, and then flip flop. I certainly don't expect a victor to emerge from the passive/active argument in my lifetime. Both investing styles have merit and both have advantages and disadvantages. Let's delve deeper …

Chapter 10

Are Markets Efficient?

"If I subscribed to the Efficient markets theory I'd still be delivering papers" – *Warren Buffett*

Most financial advisers that study finance or finance theory learn about the teachings of Professor Eugene Fama and what is called Efficient Market Hypothesis. Similar theories to EMH are the Random Walk hypothesis and the Martingale Model since effectively they all believe in the same underlying concept.

Efficient Market Hypothesis states that it is impossible to *beat the market* because stock market efficiency causes existing share prices to always reflect all relevant information. According to the EMH, stocks always trade at their fair value, making it impossible for investors to outperform the overall market through stock selection or market timing, and that the only way an investor can possibly obtain higher returns is by purchasing riskier investments.

Efficient Market believers are generally believers in Passive Investing, because they feel that since all the information is available, there is no way to gain an edge over other investors ... and therefore trying to improve your odds is a fool's errand. As long as the information is readily available to all parties, they believe that no one can have an edge over anyone else.

One of the few extreme (and illegal) contradictions is insider trading. With insider trading, obviously one person has more information than others and therefore has a potential edge on the market, but since it is illegal, Efficient Market theorists assume that this situation doesn't apply and that all markets are efficient as a result.

Active Investors obviously feel very different from this. They feel there are ways that they can gain an edge over others by using specific analysis. As I mentioned above, the jury is still out on this … some Active Investors consistently beat the market, but most have some market beating years and non-market beating years … implying that there is no consistent edge to be had.

Certainly I would say that IF markets are truly *efficient*, THEN there is no question that passive investing is the only way to invest. The reason is that the fees are less for a passively managed fund like an ETF and if there is no way to gain an edge … you might as well be in a vehicle that has the lowest fees, ultimately putting more in your pocket at the end of the day.

My personal belief is that Efficient Market theorists are leaving out a VERY important piece of information in their logic. Although all information may be out there for everyone to read therefore implying efficiency … what is NOT readily available is the *reaction* to the information from people. In other words, if good news about the economy is released and it is released fairly so that everyone gets the information at the same moment, then we would assume that the market would rise based on the good news, yet many times this clearly does not happen and we see the opposite.

> ***"The stock market moves ahead of world events. The stock market is not operating in the present, reflecting the present; it is operating on what is yet to be, the future. The market often moves contrary to apparent common sense and world events, like it had a mind of its own, designed to fool the most people, most of the time. Eventually the truth of why it moved as it did will emerge."*** - *Jesse Livermore*

A great example of this, has occurred many times this year when the economic reports were released showing better than expected growth in the US economy, and yet the market reacted negatively. Looking at this logically, a positive economic report should imply that companies will have more profit in the coming months and therefore stocks will be more valuable … i.e. rising stock market. BUT … the market actually tanked a few percentage points immediately after the reports came out. Good news is bad news and bad news is good … why??

> ***"Efficient markets' does not mean that the price of every security at every moment in time is correct."*** *– Burton Malkiel*

If markets are efficient, then good news would create a good outcome, but it doesn't always. In the above case, what has happened this year is that good news about the economy has actually caused investors to be concerned that the Federal Reserve will slow its Quantitative Easing program which many argue is helping the market rise. Without the Government pumping money into the system, many think the market will correct severely … so good news about the economy causes some to speculate that the Government will slow its' program and therefore the stock market will fall. So … good news, causes a bad result?!?!?!

As I said previously, trying to understand the impact of a *news event* is a fool's errand, trying to predict the future outcome is something that mutual funds and large brokerage houses spend billions (literally) every year in analyst fees and many times their analysis is completely incorrect. This is the main reason why most managers underperform the markets year after year, they are trying to predict what is going to happen next and most times this is just an impossible task.

> ***"The only function of economic forecasting is to make astrology look respectable."*** *- John Kenneth Galbraith*

All the information may be out there, but our *reaction* to the information will vary ... And herein lies the problem with EMH. Human behavior and the emotional reaction to events (greed and fear) cause markets to act irrationally.

The issue really has nothing to do with all information being priced into the market, but rather the market's emotional response that matters.

A great example happened in 2013 … the Boston Marathon bombing. If you remember this horrific event that was considered a terrorist attack, and yet the market basically shrugged off the event and it did not impact prices. Although there was an initial drop of a few percent, within a few days the market had recovered the loss and moved on to higher ground. I don’t want to make light of this tragedy since it was truly horrible; my heart goes out to the friends and loved ones whose lives were affected by this event. Lives were lost, a city was more or less shut down for a week … but unlike previous terror attacks on our country, financially the reaction was mooted; there was little negative impact.

If you compare the immediate reaction to attacks on 9/11, attacks on our embassies over the years, and the Boston Marathon bombing, you will see a very different reaction each time. This is quite common, where a similar news event has a very different outcome each time because of the reaction of investors.

> ***“A normal market is the kind that never really happens.”*** - *William Hamilton*

If a bombing occurs, obviously everyone has access to this information and since EMH says the market is efficient, we would assume that the market would drop … But as people react there is a period of time where the market gets out of whack. As panic sets in, and people sell, the price drops and eventually it gets back into efficiency. So, although I would agree that most periods of time the market is efficient, there are constantly smaller periods of time where the market is out of whack and needs time to factor in this new information.

The other issue is that the situation is constantly changing which can create a looping effect. If people react badly to a new event, this causes other people to reassess the situation and possibly sell their own shares, which then creates more panic and so on and so on. So, although everyone has the same information, the reaction of the masses creates a new dynamic that hasn't been factored in and quite honestly can't be.

A silly question I always pose ... does a bombing really affect the value of Coca Cola? No it doesn't, people will drink soda whether we have been bombed or not. So, is efficiency even something that matters in the market? The reason Coca Cola drops with all other stocks is because people are irrationally acting out during scary moments.

> ***"If markets were rational, I'd be waiting tables for a living"*** – *Warren Buffett*

Obviously many news events have a logical reaction by investors, but many more are not logical. How many times have you seen a company report stellar earnings and yet the stock still tanks by the end of the day? How is that possible if markets were efficient? If everyone expected great news and they got it, then why would the reaction be so negative? Human Reaction is the cause. In this particular example, which happens quite often with individual stocks, the most likely reason the stock plummets is that there is euphoria after the earnings release and as the price starts to rise, a few larger institutional investors use this as a way to exit their position. Regardless of the earnings release they decided that they wanted out of the stock and so they used this news event as an opportunity to shed their shares quickly ultimately causing a plummet in prices.

> ***"A market is the combined behavior of thousands of people responding to information, misinformation, and whim."*** *- Kenneth Chang.*

The stock market is simply supply and demand playing out over and over again. If one person wants to sell a huge chunk of shares and there are not enough buyers to absorb those shares, the price drops until there are enough interested buyers. In the case above, in a sense … we had insider trading. Not literally, but by definition the market is NOT efficient because one party knew they wanted to sell their massive lot of shares, while everyone else did not know this. To me, this puts a big hole in the idea of efficient markets. Human Behavior makes the market not efficient.

Heck, if markets were efficient then we would never have 50% drops in the value of a stock or index in a short period of time.

> ***"If you would have bought $1,000 worth of Nortel stock one year ago [2001], it would now be worth $49. $1,000 worth of Broad Vision is now worth $22. $1,000 worth of JDSU is now worth $52. Now consider this. . . If you bought $1,000 worth of Budweiser (the beer, not the stock) one year ago, drank all the beer, and traded in the cans for the nickel deposit, you would have $79."*** *- Michael Covel*

So if markets are NOT efficient, the bigger question is, can one predictively know the future, or better yet, the emotional reaction of the future. If they can, then obviously active investing is the way to go.

One could argue that certain trends cause certain industries to grow. To use the bombing example, it would be reasonable to expect firearms sales to rise immediately after a bombing or riot

… and therefore it could be a good investment. I heard on 9/11 there were a number of institutional investors that were madly trying to buy up shares of defense companies, knowing that over the next few days the general public would do the same. So, I think it is safe to say that at certain times you could theoretically have an edge, but guessing the future on a consistent basis seems farfetched. Doing it at obvious times like after a bombing … sure, but guessing what the next hot sector will be in the coming year probably isn't going to consistently pay off. Which is the main argument of passive investing, that you can't reliably predict the next turn on the roller coaster, so you might as well not try and instead just hang on for the ride.

So is Passive better? Not necessarily ... because of one huge flaw. Remember passive investing is 'buy and hold', which as you now know means 'buy and hope,' and since B&H provides absolutely zero protection, if an Active Investor places an emphasis on risk control they very likely could gain an edge.

With that said, many active managers have no risk control built in. Their primary goal is to achieve the largest profit, which unfortunately creates more risk. This is one of the reasons why small cap *riskier* stocks have done better than large cap stocks in January over the past 40ish years. There is something called, 'the January Effect' in the market, where small cap stocks outperform the larger caps for a period of months. This has been a very reliable indicator with 40 of the last 43 years proving this. The January Effect is a result of large institutional funds buying riskier stocks early in the year, knowing that if their riskier bets end up wrong they have all year to make up for the loss … since ultimately their year-end performance numbers are important to getting new investors (and getting their bonuses). So these Active Investors are taking undo risk, knowing they have time to fix the situation if something bad happens with their trades.

To me, there really is not one definitive perfect investment style between Passive Investing vs. Active Investing. Realistically neither strategy is best in all markets, since it really depends on each moment in time. Sometimes one will outperform, and other times the other style is better. In 2008, a Passive style took almost half of your portfolio away, but in 2013 the best strategy was to just 'buy and hold' … a Passive Strategy since the market just kept rising with very little correction along the way.

Ultimately the issue is less about which is better ... and more about your risk tolerance and whether it is more important to mirror the ups and downs of the market at minimal expense (Passive) or maximize gains with increased cost (Active). It really comes down to what the individual investor is most comfortable with ... To ask some very tough questions like, Are you willing to accept a 50% loss in your portfolio to potentially make a 50% gain?

With all the above said, out of the massive decline of 2008 came a new breed of active managers that focus NOT on return potential, but on risk control.

Chapter 11

Protective Investing

There is a third style that has emerged out of the massive decline of 2008 that is sort of a hybrid approach; the focus is NOT on return potential, but on risk control. Although there is not an official name to this style as of yet, I have coined it Protective Investing because it has a defensive slant to its approach. It combines elements of both Passive and Active styles with a focus on keeping your capital safe.

The term is called Protective Investment Management, and the focus is not on gains, but rather protection. They place an emphasis on preserving your original investment and know that there is a chance that as they take defensive measures they may miss a rise in the market and as a result underperform in the short-term, yet because of this defensive approach there are never any massive drops in their portfolio's value.

Protective Investors, similar to Passive Investors, believe that trying to pick the next big winning stock is a futile effort. There are just too many factors involved to try and find the next big winner and know that realistically betting on a small handful of potential stocks generally is going to be a wash over time, not making any more money than a 'buy and hold' approach. So … they invest in larger market vehicles like ETFs or Mutual Funds that move with the market as a whole and are less affected by industry or news noise. Since three out of four stocks move in the same direction as the market, this style doesn't worry about trying to find the one stock that is going to buck the trend of a declining market, but rather focuses on the general direction of the markets as a whole.

It's important to note that many Passive Investors will buy individual stocks and hold them for long periods of time, where Protective Investors only invest in whole market products (which I will explain in more detail shortly). The reason is that they know that a news event can completely crumble their portfolio when only holding a handful of stocks. An example … if the factory that makes the glass for the iPad gets flooded in a Tsunami tomorrow, Apple's stock will drop 10% - 25% as a result. Protective Investors never want to get caught in a situation like this; remember their focus is always on the defensive.

Because of this most protective investors will invest using large market ETFs or a large cap mutual fund that is not too specialized. In other words, they will make certain that the performance of one individual stock does not have the power to dramatically impact their portfolio on a day-to-day basis. They want to mirror the *market's* performance (as a whole) to minimize the chance that a single news event pulls down their portfolio.

The active elements of a protective strategy come into play with the idea that you can use historical analysis to gauge the future outcome of a situation. Remember, active investors know that they will not always be correct; they look at things in terms of probabilities and bet accordingly. If in the past a certain event occurred (i.e. a low PEG ratio) resulting in the stock going up in price 70% of the time, they are going to use that knowledge to bet more aggressively in those moments. It doesn't mean they will be right, but the odds are more in their favor than if they were to just blindly pick stocks to invest in with no analysis.

> ***"There is no perfection in trading. Instead traders must put probability in their favor."*** - *Larry Sanders*

Interestingly, this protective investment strategy is VERY popular with the ultra-affluent crowd and has been long before 2008. Ultra Wealthy investors are less concerned about making money as they are with not losing what they currently have. For them, they would much rather earn 3% a year with low risk of loss than have a potential 30% loss next year (even if it means they miss out on a 30% gain in doing so). So the protective strategies fit their style nicely knowing that they may have years of underperformance, but never a year with massive declines.

As you probably figured out already, my investing style is similar to the Protective Investing group. I feel there are pluses and minus of both Passive and Active investing styles, and therefore want a hybrid approach. I don't want to be at the whim of the market during the next major decline like Passive Investors are, but I also realize that Active Investing doesn't guarantee better performance and in fact as we have seen time and time again, most active investors actually underperform a 'buy and ~~*hold*~~ hope' strategy over time. As you will soon see, I will show you how to apply this protective approach to more than double the return of the NASDAQ, beating the Pros consistently year over year.

Chapter 12

Mutual Funds, ETFs, Stocks, Oh My!

Most people think the only way to outperform the market on a consistent basis is to (1) invest in stocks, (2) put in tons of analysis to find the next winning stock and along with this … you have to (3) be willing to take on much more risk. I've heard it so many times … more risk = more profit potential. I'm here to tell you these three statements are absolutely not correct … you do not have to take on more risk to consistently outperform the market.

I'm sure by now you are wondering what you should invest in to be able to able to almost triple the NASDAQ's return, to avoid dramatic declines in value, and most importantly not require a full time commitment, but rather require little ongoing management … only 1 minute-a-week.

If three out of four stocks move with the overall market, as we discussed in the Diversification chapter, then obviously the bigger emphasis needs to be placed, not on finding the next big winner, but rather on knowing if the market is healthy or not … and if it is then just being in (or out) at the right moments.

Since my analysis is taking a gauge of the market as a whole, I want to be investing in a whole market product that moves as closely with the market as possible. Individual stocks not only are buoyed by the market's condition, but they have their own individual news and earning issues that factor into their price movement. Whole markets tend to act more rationally than individual stocks, and for me I want the safety attributed to this. As a result, I prefer to invest in large market ETFs. You can certainly use the strategy we present in this book to find out if the market is healthy and then invest in individual stocks from there, but I prefer the safety of investing in larger products that are less at the whim of a single news event.

I have found that ETFs provide the best bang for your buck for this type of investing. ETF stands for *Exchange-Traded Fund*. They are basically mutual funds that trade like a stock, but offer transparency, tax efficiency and lower expenses.

A mutual fund is a diversified portfolio of stocks managed by an investment company. Investors purchase shares in the fund itself and make or lose money based on the combined profits and losses of the stocks the fund owns. When you put $1.00 in a mutual fund, the mutual fund company in a sense takes that $1.00 and splits it up among all the underlying stocks. So if the mutual fund owns 100 stocks, your $1.00 is split among the 100 stocks ... which in a sense gives you instant ownership to one hundred companies. The advantage of a mutual fund is that you have instant diversification. ETF's are the same in this regard, you own a basket of stocks when you invest in an ETF, but the main difference is how the stocks are picked that the fund owns.

A mutual fund picks *actively* and chooses the companies they want to invest in with the hope that they will pick winning positions and make more money than a 'buy and hold' approach. Mutual Funds use active management. They pay analysts big bucks to come up with their buy and sell decisions. The premise is that you're getting a top-notch manager who makes investment decisions for you, but this occurs at a cost. Mutual Fund fees are higher relative to a passive strategy and this eats into your profit potential. I don't want to give the impression that mutual funds are bad, because they absolutely are not. In fact, I think they are an amazing tool for people that do not want to put the time in to invest themselves OR who do not want to work with a more specialized advisor.

The one downside of mutual funds is that they are not allowed to move out of the market; they cannot 'go to cash' when things start looking ugly. So, your portfolio stays invested in the market when the market corrects. There is little downside protection while invested in a mutual fund, except for the fact that the managers may move your investments into a more defensive position so the loss is minimized.

In fact, this is why during corrections the larger, somewhat safer stocks do less bad than the smaller more risky ones. Mutual Funds need a place to park their money during volatile markets, so they try to minimize the pain by moving their money away from the smaller riskier stocks into safer large multi-national conglomerates. Their thought process is that "if the market is going to tank, at least we know that the larger companies will likely be around at the end of the correction, whereas a smaller company may or may not." Do you remember the Super Bowl ads from Pets.com and eToys.com? How about WebVan or even Netscape? Their HOPE is that they won't have to sell while the stock is a losing position on their books, and that when the market improves they will have minimized the pain during the correction.

In fact, looking at the comparison of large caps to small caps has served well as an indicator to the future direction of the market. If small caps are outperforming large caps, there generally is bullish sentiment in the market which can imply that the market is going up from that point. Whereas if suddenly there is a shift in assets from small caps to large caps and the larger caps are outperforming as a result this can imply that a correction is coming since the institutional investors are taking more defensive positions.

==

As I mentioned earlier, when you invest in an ETF, you also invest in a basket of stocks, but the difference is that an ETF tracks or mirrors a particular index instead of having a manager pick the stocks that it owns. As an example, if you invest in the SPY ETF, you are investing in the 500 companies that make up the S&P500 index. If you invest in IWM, the Russell 2000 ETF, you are investing in the 2000 companies that make up the Russell 2000 index. The ETF mirrors the index that it tracks, so if the S&P500 is up 0.4% today, the SPY will also be up roughly the same amount. If this paragraph is confusing to you, don't worry ... I discuss *indexes* in detail at the beginning of Part II.

You might want to jump ahead just to read that portion and then come back.

WHY WOULD ONE INVEST IN AN ETF INSTEAD OF A MUTUAL FUND?

Since an ETF is simply tracking an index, the companies that run the ETFs do not need to pay high analyst fees to find winning stocks and so they pass the cost savings on to you. As a result, the fees you pay are significantly lower than using a mutual fund. So you end up with more in your pocket. ETF fees are generally between 0.1% and 0.7% a year, while a mutual fund fees are usually between 1% and 3%. This sounds like a small difference, but over time this 1% difference can amount to hundreds of thousands of dollars.

Investing in an ETF is a passive strategy, it is basically a 'buy and hold' where you are not trying to outsmart the market by guessing which stocks will outperform, but rather you just want to be invested in the market as a whole.

So, we use a passive investment, but use the signals which we discuss in Part II to get us in or out of the market at opportune times. Since WE are making the buy and sell decisions, there's no need to pay higher fees to have someone decide for us like a mutual fund or financial advisor does. We in a sense are the manager; using a passive investment style, but actively watching the investment to exit when things get iffy, and of course, get back in when things look more conducive to making money.

Now, if you were not managing the account, protecting it from decline as I will teach you in Part II, then I would definitely recommend using a mutual fund instead of an ETF. Remember that an ETF is *passive* … and, as we've already discussed, a passive approach is a 'buy and ~~*hold*~~ hope' approach, with no built-in downside protection.

But if you are spending your 1 minute-a-week to monitor and protect your account, then I feel using an ETF over time is more favorable. With that said, you could use the technique presented in this book to find out when you should be invested in and out of the market, and actually have your money in a mutual fund. As an example, many of my clients have 401ks that do not allow for ETF investing, so they use our strategies and invest in a large market mutual fund which have lots of diversification in the US market. Large diversified mutual funds are generally less expensive than more actively managed mutual funds.

Chapter 13

International Investing

DO YOU NEED TO INVEST INTERNATIONALLY TO REDUCE RISK OR INCREASE MY PERFORMANCE?

Through my 100 year study, I have become particularly biased to the American market. I think there are enough opportunities here, and since most foreign indexes correlate with the US indexes, a decline here ultimately means a decline there. Another interesting discovery looking over history when comparing foreign stock market performance to the domestic market, the US market holds up better in *large* declines and recovers quicker from them.

Remember investing in foreign stocks does not lower your risk level via diversification. It can raise your profit potential but don't think that by putting 10-30% of your investment in a foreign mutual fund you are protecting yourself. In fact, you have a much higher risk on those foreign holdings since not only do you need to follow other country's market signals, you also have to closely monitor the general market of the particular country involved. Sudden changes in that country's interest rates, currency, or government policy could, through one unexpected action, wreak havoc on your investment.

Although the strategy introduced in this book will work equally well in foreign markets, I just don't feel there is a need to go there for great investment opportunities. America has always proven to be a market leading enterprise and with the country's new found oil boom and potential energy independence; I see no reason for a change anytime soon.

Chapter 14

Life Is Like a Box of Chocolates

You know the famous quote from the movie *Forrest Gump* … "Life is like a box of chocolates, you never know what you are going to get …" There has been much discussion in the investing world centered around the 'Random Walk Theory' which was introduced by Burton Malkiel in his book *A Random Walk Down Wall Street.* The book, a good read, but flawed in my opinion, remains on the top-seller list for finance books.

In short, the random walk theory is the idea that stocks take a random and unpredictable path. A follower of the random walk theory believes it's impossible to outperform the market without assuming additional risk. Critics of the theory, however, contend that stocks do maintain price trends over time - in other words, that it is possible to outperform the market by carefully selecting entry and exit points.

If you are driving down the street and you come upon an intersection with a red light, you choose to stop and wait for the light to turn green, why? Some would say they stop because they don't want to get a ticket, yet others because it is dangerous and they don't want to get in an accident.

Does this mean that you will ALWAYS get in an accident at that intersection if you run the red light, or NEVER get in an accident if you never run a red light? Of course not. I learned this the hard way when I was 21 and after waiting for a light to turn green, drove my motorcycle safely (I thought) into the intersection, only to realize as I was flying through the air after a car ran a red light and hit me, that the odds were not in my favor that day. Yet, generally speaking, we know that by obeying the traffic laws, the odds are better that we will get home safely and that there is a good *probability* that if you run that red light, something bad might happen.

> ***"History rhymes: it does not repeat."*** - *Mark Twain*

The same can be said for investing in the market. No style is 100% safe, and if anyone tries to tell their strategy is "guaranteed" … you should run from them quickly. There are just too many factors in the market to be able to guarantee the outcome, and the reality is that these factors change from minute to minute. As I write this, the market is flirting with a multi-year high, yet if we wake up tomorrow and someone has decided to hijack a plane and fly it into the White House, obviously all bets are off as it's likely that no one's portfolio is safe. Yet, the odds that this will happen tomorrow are obviously slim and therefore we should *bet* accordingly.

If you look at the best traders in history, they use probabilities to help their decision process. Is it possible that we will be attacked tomorrow? Sure, but is it likely? Of course not. I know this is a silly example, but the point here is that we can and should make sound judgments based on history to help our decision process.

> ***"Another lesson I learned early is that there is nothing new in Wall Street. There can't be because speculation is as old as the hills. Whatever happens in the stock market today has happened before and will happen again."*** - *Jesse Livermore*

When everyone is panicking and selling, like they did in 2008 what were the best traders doing? They were keeping their cool and buying up everything because they knew that the odds were that things will get better shortly. Look at Warren Buffett who invested billions into Bank of America in 2011 at a time when we all thought all banks were going to go under due to the mortgage crisis.

Fear has a funny way to making us as humans throw all logic out the window. We think that the current crisis is *the new norm* and that there is no chance we will ever get out of the current mess we are in. Even as we try to use logic to quell our concerns, it takes an incredibly strong individual to overpower our panicked minds. Yet using history as a guide we can obviously look logically at the current situation to assess the likely outcome. If over the last 10,000 days we were attacked on only one day, you could argue that tomorrow we have a 1 in 10,000 chance of being attacked. The odds are definitely that we will NOT be attacked. The bottom line is that, there will ALWAYS be some newsworthy event to panic over … a reason to say "this time it's different," yet, using history we can look at the likely outcome and act accordingly.

Wall Street would have you believe that the market moves randomly, and there is no way to anticipate the future outcome and while this is partly true, there are clear ways to move the odds in your favor, to increase the probability that you will outperform the general averages.

So how do you do this? The first rule in investing is to leave your emotions outside. Most active investors severely underperform a 'buy and hold' approach simply because they let their emotions play a role in the trading decision. In fact, when I started this endeavor 10-ish years ago, I knew this was going to be my biggest hurdle in creating a successful strategy. I knew myself well enough to know that I reacted to news events at the worst possible time even if I could logically prove via historical analysis that my worst fears were unfounded. I needed a way to remove my emotion from the process, and minimizing the noise in my head was the quickest way to do this. As a result, my very first decision was to turn off the news.

> ***"Tune out the financial TV channels. Watch the cooking channel or the gardening channel if you want useful advice."*** - *Burton Malkiel*

Most people think the news will provide some insight into the market's future direction, but let's be honest, if the newscasters really knew what they were doing would they be reporting the news OR sitting on an island lighting cigars with $100 bills? Or at least they would be on Wall Street putting their knowledge to good use. Their job is to keep you watching, not to make you money ... and by creating fear at the worst moments or euphoria at the best moments they increase their viewership. I don't want to imply newscasters are bad people because they're obviously not, but watching the news will NOT help your portfolio in any way. Generally speaking the worst news headlines are at the very bottom of a decline, and the best at the very top.

"There is no greater kiss of death like seeing a bull on the cover of Time." - *Barron magazine*

Legg Mason strategist Paul MacRae Montgomery, the originator of the *Magazine Cover Indicator*, showed that once a magazine cover such as *Time* or *Newsweek* features a bullish statement on a financial trend, we were close to or already at a major market top, and when it implied the market was going to keep falling (a bearish cover), we were generally at the very bottom. Buy High and Sell Low ... not the best trading style for sure.

Okay, so all this proves what some savvy Wall Street soothsayers have long known; that magazine covers are poor predictors of subsequent performance. The question is, why? Are magazines just bad at business? Are journalists just bad at identifying good and bad companies? The answer will actually get your favorite magazines and journalists off the hook for being poor stock market prognosticators.

If you think about what it takes to move a story from an idea to cover you begin to see why the market has already moved on by the time the magazine's current issue has gone to press. After all, magazines like to pursue cover stories that hold broad appeal.

They are looking for ways to sell the most copies possible, and what better way to do this, than to publish articles that hold mainstream popularity. Whether the cover has Lady Ga Ga or Apple's most recent iPhone the reason for the placement is the same; because it's hot, people dig it, they want to know more about it, and the image sells.

> ***"We have two classes of forecasters: Those who don't know and those who don't know they don't know."*** *- John Kenneth Galbraith*

If you are not able to remove your emotions from your investment decisions, then a 'buy and hold' approach is probably the best solution for you. Because generally speaking, people that take an active approach to investing underperform a 'buy and hold' approach simply because they make emotional decisions at the worst possible moment. In fact, this might be the only good reason why hiring a professional to manage your investments might make sense, simply because they can leave emotion out of the decision process and more easily look at the investment with a probabilities perspective.

> ***"Good traders need confidence; they need discipline; and the confidence to rigidly stick to their discipline."*** *- Tom Peterson*

Bottom line, you must find a way to remove your emotions from your investment decisions if you are going to be successful in the market.

Chapter 15

Never Name Your Animals

"Forget your ego, swallow your pride, stop trying to argue with the market, and don't get emotionally attached to any stock that's losing you money. Remember: there are no good stocks; they're all bad … unless they go up in price" *William O'Neil from How to Make Money in Stocks*

My wife and I have close friends that own a large ranch in Montana. Visiting them is so surreal for me; you see I'm a city boy. Born and raised in the city and never spent a day outside of one. I'm pretty wimpy when it comes to all of that survival stuff, never been camping where there wasn't a porta-potty close by, never had to hunt for food, never been hiking where there weren't signs posted to keep me out of danger, etc. So seeing this alternate lifestyle that my 'farm friends' have is always an eye opener for me.

They live really remote, the nearest rinky dink 'town' is 30 minutes away with only a general store and gas station. There is no Super Target, Costco, Fashion Square mall, and most important for señor wimp-i-ness (that's me) … no hospital … you have to drive 2 hours to get to those.

They grow some crop, but mostly they are meat ranchers … they raise cows and sheep with the eventual goal to sell these animals for the meat that we see in our grocery stores. What is interesting is that the thought of mirroring their life really appeals to me, but whenever I go down that road in my head I quickly get a reality check … I'd be dead after one winter. Like I said, I'm just a wimpy city boy.

These are some tough folk (although when talking to them, you would never guess it). They have to 'put down' sick animals, actually leave the warm house when it is 30 below zero to make certain the animal's water isn't frozen, shoot coyotes and other predators that try to kill their animals. Heck … they even have to do that thing in *City Slickers* when Billy Crystal's character is helping to deliver a calf and the baby gets stuck and the only solution is to go '*arms deep*.'

I told you … I'd die!

The kicker … they even built their house with their own hands! And this is no ordinary house, it is REALLY nice. Do you know what my 'house' would look like if I built it myself?!?! I attempted to build my kids play structure a few years back and after a few hours sent my wife rushing to the store to get Band-Aids and anti-bacterials. That play structure took me about a month to build, and I still get nervous to this day when the boys get on the second story and start jumping on the floor boards … not sure if that thing is going to hold.

I always joke with my wife that if World War III happens, when we flee the city we're 'going to the farm.' Which is a joke in its' own right, what good would I be to them?? I can see it now, as he is holding a shot gun protecting his property and she has her pink-handled Glock pointed at me … and I try to tell them how I can work a spreadsheet like nobody's business, and that I'm really good with numbers, but if I get a blister on my hand I'm going to cry like a baby. Man, this story is just depressing me … I really am a wimp!!

I could sum up their life in exactly 30 seconds. You know those "Ford Tough" or Chevy "Like a Rock" commercials? Get the picture now? These people are tough. I personally am not "like a rock" … when I play rock-paper-scissors with my kids; I'm more like the 'paper.'

I realize I am painting the picture of Neanderthal people, but here's the kicker, these are the nicest, most loving people I have ever met, and their dedication and loyalty to their family is just unprecedented. They have 7 daughters; yes you read that right …

7! The youngest are only 2 (twins like our youngest) and the oldest is 13.

I will always remember the first time I drove up to their house (I had heard a lot about them through my wife before I actually met them). My first thought was … "Wow, this is a real farm." They have a few thousand acres of land, with massive grain silos and tons of tractor equipment, a real farm.

This visit really opened my eyes to what a sheltered life I live. They had asked if our boys (5 years old at the time) wanted to feed the baby pigs, and we of course could barely contain our excitement. I mean, what 5-year-old doesn't want to get in a pig pen and run around with baby piglets. So, we walked over to the barn where roughly 30 piglets were waiting for dinner. The event was a hoot to watch; the boys chasing the pigs around the paddock trying to corral them into the feeding area … I can still hear the banjo music playing in my head as the pigs outsmarted my boys each and every time.

In any case, as we were walking back to the house I was talking with their oldest daughter and we came upon a sick lamb; on the ground, looking up, very little life left in it. She bent down and lightly pet the face of the lamb. It seemed pretty obvious even with my limited knowledge of animal husbandry that the lamb was probably not going to make it through the night, it was very sick. We stood there for a few minutes and eventually she started walking away, to which I followed. Both of us were very quiet, and I eventually broke the silence and asked "was that hard for you to see?" To which she quickly answered with a no. We eventually changed conversation and continued on our path back to the house.

That moment was VERY hard for me. I really had never encountered a dying animal and my first impulse was to try to save the animal, to do everything in my power to bring it back to life. Yet her life experience even with as young as she was, was very different than mine. When we were standing over the lamb, I watched her intently trying to gain a clue as to what she was feeling. She knew through her experience that animals die sometimes and that you simply can't stop it. I found out later that the lamb had a disease and that they had given the proper medicine but there was nothing more that could have been done.

It boggled my mind to think about this 13-year-old and how hard it must have been for her to experience that moment, but I later realized that … no … she was fine with it; I was the one that was having a hard time. She had been raised in this lifestyle and had dealt with dying animals before, it was just a part of life … and yet I, 4 times her age had not embraced the idea that death was as common as birth. When you raise thousands of animals, you unfortunately are going to have a few that are just not going to make it.

I later was talking to her dad while flipping burgers and I mentioned the lamb that we had stumbled upon and how impressed I was with his oldest daughter's reaction. He said something that I'll always remember to this day, "*You don't name your animals.*" At first, I didn't understand what he meant by this comment, but on the drive home it became clear.

He was running a business here, just as I run my business, and his business was there to feed his family, to provide for them, just like mine. And in order to do that, he needed to treat every decision as a business one; there was no room for emotion. It might sound callous, but a business by definition exists to be profitable, to benefit the shareholders which in his case was his family. His business was not unlike most out there … you buy raw materials, you alter them in some way, and then you sell the finished product. He had baby sheep and calf, fed and took care of them with the eventual goal to sell them. This was a business.

When I stood over that dying lamb, I could not remove the emotion from the moment. His daughter saw the lamb for what it was, although we both understood how tragic that moment was, they were running a business and to be successful you have to be emotionless. All businesses have loss and she understood that, I on the other hand did not.

"You don't name your animals" ... You never fall in love with the stocks you own. If you are going to be successful in the stock market, you must NEVER get emotional. Making money in the market and more importantly protecting your money is serious business and the day you realize this and act accordingly is the day you will start doing well in the market.

If there is only one thing that you take away from this book it is to *never name your animals*! Never let emotion dictate your actions, treat investing like a business. You are up against the most intelligent people out there that are way smarter, have way more resources, and quite honestly want nothing more than to clean out your wallet. Your loss is their gain. Stop acting with your emotions, and start acting logically.

Chapter 16

Simon Says

> ***"I believe that having the discipline to follow your rules is essential. Without specific, clear, and tested rules, speculators do not have any real chance of success. Why? Because speculators without a plan are like a general without a strategy, and therefore without an actionable battle plan. Speculators without a single clear plan can only act and react, act and react, to the slings and arrows of stock market misfortune, until they are defeated."*** *- Jesse Livermore*

So, how do you take an active approach to investing, but keep your emotions out of the process? It's actually quite simple. You need to setup rules for yourself. If A occurs, you will do B.

The only way to beat the market consistently is to have a rule-based system that will protect you when price is showing weakness, and get you in only when the situation is optimal for profit.

Just like the red light example above, you know that if you choose to run the red light, you are breaking the rules and you might have to pay a consequence. It doesn't matter whether you are late for work or late for dinner, or whatever … you follow the rule. Sure, you might end up home from work a few minutes sooner, but you also know that the odds are against you and that something bad will likely happen if you drive through that intersection.

For me, I knew that the only way to create a successful system for myself was that it had to be rule-based and emotionless. Entry and exit decisions needed to be based on historical precedent, and not on my emotional whims.

In fact, this is the only way to succeed consistently in the market. You need to get the odds in your favor and act accordingly, and the only way to do this is to develop a rule-based system that when X happens, you will do Y.

By looking at history and comparing it to the current environment, we are able to get a gauge for what may happen next. Why is this, because we as humans really haven't changed much over the past hundred years, we are still motivated primarily by fear and greed, and we base our decisions on survival. So, although the news event might be different, our reaction to it is generally the same.

> ***"The game does not change and neither does human nature."*** *- Jesse Livermore*

Now, before you get all up in arms that "just because it happened in the past, doesn't mean it will happen in the future," I want to point out that our entire thought process as a civilization is based on using historical precedent to predict a future outcome. In fact, our brains are even oriented to think this way. If a baby cries he gets the attention of his mother, so what does he do? He cries more often. He has learned by analyzing history that crying gets what he wants.

Statistics is "the practice or science of collecting and analyzing numerical data in large quantities." It provides a way to study history to create a probability that the same outcome will happen again in the future. A statistician's goal is the find out what 'the norm' looks like and through that analysis they can predict the odds that something will happen again.

If you think about it, most of our modern civilization is designed around statistical studies. Our traffic laws are based on statistics. Traffic accidents and traffic-related fatalities increase as the speed limit increases and as a result, speed limits have been established at specific levels to maximize safety.

Statistics are used everywhere, and the common idea is to use past history to gain an assessment on future direction. Airplane manufacturers use historical studies to find the best materials to keep planes and rockets in the air. College acceptance is based on the results on the SAT and ACT exams. The IRS uses statistics to analyze tax returns to find the few that have a high probability that they contain fraudulent information. Even the Secret Service uses historical analysis to help protect the President.

Someone quipped above, "just because something happened in the past does not mean it will happen again in the future," and that's potentially true. One of the biggest problems with using historical analysis for anything is related to 'data fitting.' Data fitting occurs when an assumption is made about the future outcome based on past precedent without large enough historical samples. If something happened 50 times before, there is a good chance it will happen again. Right? Well not necessarily. If you flip a quarter 10 times and it shows up heads 9 times, one could suggest that there is a 90% chance that when you flip that same coin again it will come back as heads. But, we all see the problem here.

Making assumptions using small data sets is obviously a significant issue. So how does a person get around this problem? A good analyst will start with a theory and then test it, and if the theory holds up, they test it further with larger and larger data sets. To me, a strategy regardless of its' technique is successful only if it is consistent and performs as expected across all time periods.

In our case at Resnn, we have tested our systems through the past 40 years of history, seeing the performance through extreme periods of time like hyper inflation in the 70s, the dramatic decline in October 1987, The Persian Gulf War, dot-com bubble, 9/11 and so on. The goal was to identify times where the model did not perform as expected, and to be able to help customers gain an expectation of their future performance. Testing through 40 years was not easy for sure, but a good strategy uses enough data to identify times where the system performs well and where it doesn't.

By testing through 40 years, does this mean that we found the Holy Grail, the perfect investing solution that can predict every possible outcome in the future? Absolutely not! Statistics do not guarantee future success, but the more analysis performed, the more likely the future outcome will be as expected.

> ***"Regarding learning from your mistakes, the best thing to do is to learn from the other guy's mistakes. As Patton used to say, 'It's an honor to die for your country, but make sure the other guys get the honor.' Our approach is really to try and learn vicariously."*** *- Warren Buffett*

To use the above examples, just because someone is driving at 120 mph doesn't guarantee they will crash, and on the opposite side, driving at 30 mph isn't necessarily more safe, but historically a maximum speed of 55 mph to 75 mph is a *good* freeway speed that minimizes traffic related accidents while keeping the flow of traffic reasonable. For SAT's, a perfect score doesn't necessarily imply future success, but looking at the data statistically shows that the odds are in that person's favor. So, although there are no guarantees by using statistical analysis, historical precedent puts the odds in your favor, and that's what it is all about … using empirical data to increase your probability of success.

By creating rules based on historical precedent, you can quite simply put the odds in your favor. There will be times when the outcome will not be what historically occurred, but by putting the odds in your favor you will be right more than wrong.

> ***"In this business, if you're good, you're right six times out of ten. You're never going to be right nine times out of ten."*** *– Peter Lynch*

Quite honestly, you don't have to be right too often to outperform the markets. In fact, the strategy introduced in Part II, the one that doubled (almost tripled) a 'buy and ~~*hold*~~ hope' approach has a win rate of only 47%! That means it is wrong more than right. How can that be?? How can you be wrong more than 50% of the time and still make money?

I list every trade in the appendix over the past 41 years, and what you will see is that when we are right (when the trade is acting well and making us money) … on average we stay in the trade for a long time. We are in the market for over half the year on our most successful trades, and averaging all our profitable trades the average time in the market is 83 trading days (roughly 4 1/2 months).

Yet, what is most interesting is with our losing trades. While we have more of them, our average losing trade keeps us in the market only 17 trading days (less than 1 month). **It is okay to be wrong, it is not ok to stay wrong.**

Remember … It doesn't matter that you are right, just that you make money. If you have trouble being wrong, then the stock market is not a place for you. You need to leave your ego at the door.

Most full time and institutional traders consider a 50% win rate to be quite exceptional, and 60% is just unheard of. In fact, I have some trading buddies that have less than a 30% success rate (they are wrong on their trades 70% of the time!!) yet they are wildly successful, because their rules get them in when the odds are in their favor and more importantly, protect them when they were wrong.

> ***"The basic concept that applies to both poker and trading is that the primary object is not winning the most hands, but rather maximizing your gains." - Jeff Yass***

How can one be right less than half the time and still make money? Imagine if you went to Las Vegas and placed 10 bets. Of those 10 bets, you had 9 losing bets where you bet $10.00 each time (a loss of $90.00), but on the final bet, you decided to risk everything and you put down a crisp $100.00 bill … and low and behold you win. Although you only had a 10% win rate (losing 9 times out of 10), you walk away with a $10.00 profit. If your winning trades earn more than your losing trades, you end up ahead of the game.

Bets	Amount Bet	Win or Loss	Account Balance
starting balance:			**$200.00**
1	$ 10.00	loss	$190.00
2	$ 10.00	loss	$180.00
3	$ 10.00	loss	$170.00
4	$ 10.00	loss	$160.00
5	$ 10.00	loss	$150.00
6	$ 10.00	loss	$140.00
7	$ 10.00	loss	$130.00
8	$ 10.00	loss	$120.00
9	$ 10.00	loss	$110.00
10	**$100.00**	**win**	**$210.00**

Using the strategy in Part II, our average winning trade returned 12%, while our average losing trade only lost 2.8%. So this means we technically can lose 4 times in a row to every one win and still make a little bit of money (2.8% x 4 = 11.4%, which is still less than 12%). This means that technically we can have as low as a 25% win rate and still make money.

This is imperative to understand and embrace. How often you are right is less important than how much damage is done when you are wrong. Creating clear cut rules to protect your portfolio from downside risk is essential for long-term success in the market.

"Letting losses run is the most serious mistake made by most investors." *- William O'Neil*

Chapter 17

The Right Time to Sell

> ***"When you feel like bragging, it's probably time to sell."*** *– John Neff*

One of 'buy and ~~*hold*~~ hope's' fundamental problems is that there are no clear cut rules for when to sell. Everyone loves to buy, but nobody wants to sell … ESPECIALLY when they are wrong. For starters, selling takes work … worrying about tax ramifications, where the money needs to go, or what to invest in now, etc. It requires work and as a result, most people hold much longer than they should. Certainly it is easy to justify holding on to a loser as a result. What was a bragging point at last year's Christmas party is now an embarrassment never to be discussed again as you hold a stock that rose nicely and then fell with the market taking your profits with it.

> ***"Trading is like (being in a) relationship – getting in is easy, but the hard part is getting out."*** *- Peter Borish*

Rules will help you with this challenge. If you follow the rules, you will NEVER be caught in a situation where your stock is down 20%, 30%, or more.

Imagine a stock at $50.00 that you own and love being invested in (warning … emotional decision here!!), as the stock drops down to $45.00, most investor's initial reaction is to buy more. "Heck, if it was a good deal at $50.00, then it's a great deal at $45.00." As the price continues to drop to $40.00 … the same outcome happens. Now the stock is 20% off … "what a discount! Buy more!" But the truth is, there no reason why the stock can't continue falling, EVEN IF it is a GREAT company.

In mid 2000, Cisco Systems … the poster child for the dot-com bull market, hit a high of $87.00 a share. As the market rolled over, many investors bought the stock on the way down at $70.00, $60.00, $50.00 and lower. Seven months later, the stock had sunk to $13.00 a share, an 80% decline for those that bought at $70.00.

Sure, Cisco was a dot-com'mer … maybe that was too risky for your blood and you prefer the safety of the Blue Chips? No safety there as well … Who would have projected that General Motors would sell for $2 a share, down from $94? AT&T hit a high of $75.00 in 1964; it took 20 years to come back to break-even. Lucent Technologies, a spin off from AT&T in the mid-1990s, hit a high of $86.25, today it trades at $4.21, 14 years later. Bank of America in 2006 was trading for $55.00 a share, two years later it was trading for $6.00, even today it has only recovered a small fraction of its' original value, trading for $16.00, a 70% loss over 8 years. Don't think there is safety in large *stable* companies, use your rules to exit when there is weakness irrespective of how safe you *think* the situation is, because history has shown time and time again that no company no matter how great or grand is free from massive decline.

> ***"Never argue with the market. Your health and peace of mind are always more important than any stock"*** – *William O'Neil*

I know it is hard to pull the trigger as a stock is declining … to sell and take a loss, but small losses are cheap insurance. If the stock reverses and moves up after you sell it, as sometimes it does, you can ALWAYS buy it back. Taking a small loss will ensure long-term survival in the market. I can't emphasize this enough, remember if you're portfolio declines in value by 50%, you have to make a 100% return just to get back to break-even … a tough task for sure. Keeping your losses small is the key to success in the market and developing rules to do this will make it easy to overcome any psychological barriers you may have over this.

> ***"Trading is a game of probabilities. You don't have to be right every time. You just have to follow your rules"*** *- Vadym Graifer & Christopher Schumacher, Techniques of Tape Reading*

So, when should you sell? Are there opportune times? After a certain level of profit or certain amount of time? The easy answer is … you don't need to worry about this. The longer answer … sometimes you will be invested only four or five days before exiting, and other times you will be in the market for a year or more. The important thing to know for now is that, the market will tell you when it's time to exit. If you enter the market and you quickly discover that you were wrong, the worst thing to do is to sit and hope things will change … nine times out of ten they won't, and your loss will become an even greater loss. In Part II, I give you the tools to know the exact moment of time that you should exit AND conversely the exact moment of time to enter.

> ***"It is incredible how rich you can get by not being perfect."*** *- Larry Hite*

The following silly story is quoted from the book, The Psychology of Speculation by Fred C. Kelly

> *A little boy was walking down the road when he came upon an old man trying to catch wild turkeys. The man had a turkey trap, a crude device consisting of a big box with the door hinged at the top. This door was kept open by a prop, to which was tied a piece of twine leading back a hundred feet or more to the operator. A thin trail of corn scattered along a path lured turkeys to the box.*
>
> *Once they were inside, the turkeys found an even more plentiful supply of corn. When enough*

> *turkeys had wandered into the box, the old man would jerk away the prop and let the door fall shut. Having once shut the door, he couldn't open it again without going up to the box, and this would scare away any turkeys that were lurking outside. The time to pull away the prop was when as many turkeys as one could reasonably expect were inside.*
>
> *One day he had a dozen turkeys in his box. Then one sauntered out, leaving 11. "Gosh, I wish I had pulled the string when all 12 were there," said the old man. "I'll wait a minute and maybe the other one will go back." While he waited for the twelfth turkey to return, two more walked out on him. "I should have been satisfied with 11," the trapper said. "Just as soon as I get one more back, I'll pull the string." Three more walked out, and still the man waited. Having once had 12 turkeys, he disliked going home with less than 8.*
>
> *He couldn't give up the idea that some of the original turkeys would return. When finally there was only one turkey left in the trap, he said, "I'll wait until he walks out or another goes in, and then I'll quit." The solitary turkey went to join the others, and the man returned empty-handed.*
>
> *The psychology of normal investors is not much different. They hope more turkeys will return to the box when they should fear that all the turkeys could walk out and they'll be left with nothing.*

The point is, you need to have a definitive plan as to when it is the right time to enter the market, and the right time to exit, but the duration will be different every time. Bottom line is that if the trade is working out, and you are making money … then you stay invested. As we saw in 1998-1999 and somewhat so in today's market in 2013, regardless of the worry in the news … a market can continue higher much longer than anyone can predict.

So you let the market tell you when it's time to exit. You don't decide, the market decides for you. As long as it is acting healthy you stay invested enjoying more and more profit, but as the market starts to change its' character and roll over … starting to decline, you exit quickly and lock in your profits. It doesn't matter that the market only dropped 2% from the high and people on TV are saying it's a bargain now … you exit. The first definitive sign of weakness is your sign to say goodbye, and the same is true for when it is time to get back in.

The rules we have setup will tell you when to enter the market, to maximize your potential. You simply need to follow the rule and not second guess it. Remember, usually when things look most grim we are at the moment in time when the greatest profit is possible. This is why Warren Buffett has done so well in his investing career, he buys beat down companies when everyone else is running for the hills and holds them until everyone else is euphoric about them. Using rules will keep you from second guessing your entry (or exit) regardless of what you are seeing on the news or hearing from your friends.

> ***"Bulls make money and bears make money, but pigs get slaughtered"*** *- Unknown*

Don't be a Pig; don't hesitate an entry or an exit. Remember you will be wrong sometimes, but all that matters in the end is that you make money. An exit at a *wrong* time means you miss out on some profit, but an exit at the *right* time means you will miss out on a large decline … **which would you prefer?**

> ***"There is the plain fool who does the wrong thing at all times anywhere, but there is the Wall Street fool who thinks he must trade all the time."*** *– Jesse Livermore*

Chapter 18

When Should You Not Be Invested?

"Sometimes your best investments are the ones you don't make." *- Donald Trump.*

When the market is not healthy, you should not be invested, period. For me, this was one of the hardest concepts to grasp in my early years. In fact, as you will see from the trades in the appendix, using the strategy in this book, you will be out of the market almost 40% of the time (since 1973, this strategy has been in the market 62% of the time).

Huh??? How can you more than double the return of the market while not being invested in it 40% of the time? As I'm sure you know the market moves in waves. It doesn't just go up, but goes up and down over cycles of time. In fact, Wall Street has coined the 2000's decade as "the Lost Decade," because it started and ended at the exact same price point ... resulting in a total gain over 10 years of 0%, but if you had been invested in a 'buy and hold' strategy for just 1999 (one year only), you would have returned over 80%. Obviously there seems to be no rhyme or reason to the cycles that occur, but clearly there are opportune times to be in the market vs. not.

"Remember, you do not have to be in the market all the time." *- Jesse Livermore*

As you will see in the next section, our strategy will get you in the market when it is ripe for rising, and get you out of the market when it appears to be ready to decline. I realize entering and exiting the market and more importantly staying out for extended periods of time seems like a strange concept. **Isn't the point of investing to profit? And how can I profit if I'm not invested?** Very good questions that deserves equally good answers.

When I was in college, I had a roommate that had a knack for gambling. He played 21, and spent most of his weeknight's playing cards, practicing so that on the weekend he could drive out to Las Vegas and hopefully turn the odds in his favor. As you know, Las Vegas games are skewed so that the odds are against you. Obviously if they were skewed in *your* favor, the casinos would quickly go out of business. Most people that go to Las Vegas don't want to look at these games as mathematical equations and probability based, but they clearly are, and you can increase your odds by betting at the right moments.

My roommate was a card-counter and although the odds are clearly against you he seemed to do pretty well. So one time I decided to go along for the ride to watch and partake as well. I was only 19 when I made my first trip with my roommate; the Las Vegas experience is so surreal for a young person. As you know with card counting, the goal is to count the high cards and low cards so that you know when there is a greater probability that a specific card will be turned over next. The goal is to ultimately bet at opportune times, when you have an increased chance of winning. If you need a high numbered card and you know that a lot of low numbers have recently been played, you can increase your bet … knowing that the odds are more in your favor.

When we got to Las Vegas, we immediately went to the floor of one of the casinos and my roommate picked a table and just sat and watched the table for about 15 minutes. I finally asked if we were going to play, and he pretty much ignored my question, but eventually he hopped in and played a number of winning hands. Then suddenly, he said he was done for awhile. Over that weekend, the pattern continued, we actually spent more time watching rather than playing. Eventually I asked him what he was doing, and he explained the obvious … "there are times when the opportunity is there to make money and that's when I play, and there are times when the odds are not in my favor, and the only safe place to be is not playing." Once I sat and thought about it this concept became obvious to me, but even after being obvious I found it was still really hard to sit and watch from the sidelines, not playing the game.

> ***"You've got to know when to hold them, know when to fold them, know when to walk away, know when to run"*** *- Kenny Rogers, The Gambler*

I hate to say it, but similar to Las Vegas, investing in the market, the odds are against you. You are up against some of the greatest financial minds (and computers) in the world, and if you are not going to play the game right, you might as well cash your entire retirement account and take it to Vegas.

There are times when the market is healthy and you should be invested, and times when it is not and you shouldn't even try to play the game. From mid 1999 until December 2001, the Resnn strategy stayed completely out of the market the entire time. For almost 2 ½ years, we sat in cash. That's A LONG time! But, what was the alternative. In 2000 the NASDAQ returned -39.3%, in 2001 the NASDAQ lost again … another 21.1%. 'Buy and ~~*hold*~~ hope' for those 2 years, resulted in a net loss of over half of your portfolio (52%).

Much as my friend taught me about Las Vegas, the same rules apply to Wall Street. When the market is not healthy, it is ok to *not* take part in it. In fact, you MUST *not* take part, it is critical to your long-term success.

> ***When the odds are not in your favor, don't even try to play the game … you will lose.***

Bottom line; don't get antsy when sitting out of the market for extended periods of time. The strategy will get you in the market when it is ready to rise and keep you safe when things are questionable. Regardless of whether it takes 5 days or 5 years for the market to stabilize after a decline to be safe to enter again, you need to understand that sometimes it is better to not play the game at all than to play when the odds are against you.

> ***"It never was my thinking that made the big money for me. It always was my sitting. Got that? My sitting tight!"*** *- Jesse Livermore, as quoted from Reminiscences of a Stock Operator, 1923.*

One final note, the other advantage of being in cash 40% of the time is that you experience a significantly lower risk level than the average investor. Sitting in cash protects you from any catastrophic event that will push the market down fast, so if you can only be invested 60% of the time and still outperform … then this should be a no brainer; take the lowest risk path.

PART II

The Winning Strategy

Ok, you've waited long enough, waded through all my boring stories and anecdotes, I suppose I've taken advantage of your time long enough … it's time to show you *the Magic Formula* … the strategy that has more than doubled the market averages over the past 40 years, and more importantly, keeps you safe from all major declines by spending only 1 minute-a-week.

For those of you that are new to Technical Analysis, I need to define and introduce some important concepts first, the nuts and bolts as I like to call them. If you are familiar with investing and specifically analyzing stocks on a chart, you can probably skip the next few chapters, although I suppose a little review couldn't hurt regardless.

Although I could simply tell you the winning strategy, I feel it is important that you thoroughly understand how it works, why it works, along with its' advantages AND disadvantages. Before you accept my (or anyone's) words, you must *Trust, but Verify*. Your understanding of the strategy and not blindly following is what will keep you ahead of the masses in the financial world.

So … let's dig in …

Chapter 19

Tracking the NASDAQ

As you recall, our first goal in investing is to find out if the market as a whole is healthy, since we only want to be invested during those times … and we can achieve that quite quickly on a daily basis by looking at the behavior of the major indexes (Dow Jones, Standard & Poors 500 Composite Index (S&P500, or just S&P for short), New York Stock Exchange Index (NYSE), Nasdaq, and Russell 2000).

This is an overly simplified definition, but the way an index works, is it takes the gains or losses of each stock that it tracks and then it averages the daily gain or loss with all the other companies in the index to arrive at the performance for the index itself. When you are driving home at night and you hear that "the S & P Composite was up 1% for the day," what that really means is that the average gain across all the companies that are tracked on the S & P was 1%. Many of those companies will be down significantly and many will be up much more than 1% for the day, but the average gain was 1%.

For reference, the S&P 500 tracks 500 companies, while the Nasdaq composites has a bit over 3,000, the Russell 2000 tracks (you guessed it …) 2,000 stocks, the NYSE tracks roughly 2,800 companies and the Dow Jones tracks only 30. Since we are looking to get a gauge of the market as a whole, ideally we want to use an index that has a large group of stocks in many sectors that move closely with the market as it ebbs and flows.

After many years of testing different indexes, I have found that the Nasdaq Composite is the best index to use in determining the health of the overall market, primarily because it correlates so well. As I mentioned above, by watching the NASDAQ, you are watching the performance of over 3,000 companies that are of varying sizes, sectors and world players. To me, it doesn't get better than this, one place to look in order to get a litmus test on the state of the market as a whole.

It is important to note that there has never been a time in history when the overall market corrected and the NASDAQ didn't lead the way or at the very least quickly follow suit, and vice versa … when the market completes a correction and starts a new uptrend the NASDAQ is right there with the rest of the market. As you will see shortly, most times the NASDAQ leads the rest of the market which ultimately means you can have a slight jump by watching this index solely. In fact, this is really the only index you need to watch in order to gain important clues as to whether it is time to act defensively or aggressively with your portfolio, hence why it takes less than 1 minute-a-week.

For those of you that are new to the stock market, let's start with a broad definition of the NASDAQ, then we will get into more specifics as to why I feel it is the only indicator you need to watch.

Although these breakdowns change slightly over time, you can get a feel for the components that make up the NASDAQ by looking at the following sector allocation:

Information Technology 51.87%

Consumer Discretionary 14.45%

Health Care 14.34%

Financials 7.72%

Industrials 5.58%

Consumer Staples 1.86%

Telecommunication Services 1.62%

Energy 1.34%

Materials 1.12%

Utilities 0.08%

The Nasdaq Composite calculates its' performance slightly differently than what I describe above, it doesn't take a straight average but rather it is a 'capitalization-weighted' index, with each company weighting being proportionate to its market value. This means that the larger the company (based on market value

… share price * number of shares outstanding), the heavier it is weighted in calculating the index. In other words, a larger company has more influence on the performance of the NASDAQ than a smaller company. Our goal in watching an index is to get a gauge of the health of the overall market, so larger companies having a larger influence are good for our purposes since we don't want a small company incorrectly swaying our analysis. In fact the Top 10 NASDAQ Composite components usually represent between 30% and 35% of the overall portfolio. At the time of this writing the top 10 components are listed below (as of January 2014).

Apple Inc.

Google Inc.

Microsoft Corporation

Amazon.com, Inc.

Facebook, Inc.

Comcast Corporation

Intel Corporation

Qualcomm Incorporated

Cisco Systems, Inc.

Although U.S. based companies represent around 90% of the index, which technically means that by investing in the NASDAQ you have 10% of your assets invested in foreign companies, as you see from the list above, these are massive, massive conglomerates that derive much of their income from overseas. So, although technically most companies in the NASDAQ are U.S. based, by investing in the underlying companies you are diversifying internationally. You can bet that Apple's quarterly financials would be negatively affected, if Europe goes into a recession.

The S&P 500 and NYSE also contain a broad spectrum of industry sectors and company sizes, but I prefer watching the NASDAQ for its' high growth focus. You probably noticed from the top 10 list that there is clearly a technology emphasis.

Companies on the NASDAQ tend to be more speculative and risky than those listed on the others and because of this, the NASDAQ composite index tends to be more volatile than other broad indexes which I look at as a bonus. Remember we are using this index to get a gauge on the health of the market, and more volatility means more obvious clues when things start going south.

In fact, large institutional funds tend to invest in riskier companies when they feel the market is healthy and will be for awhile into the future, and conversely when they start getting nervous about the state of the market, they generally exit the more risky investments and move their assets to larger *more stable* blue chips. What this means for us is that the riskier growth oriented companies usually take a hit before the larger more stable companies see any negative performance … and so by tracking higher risk portions of the market, many times we can get some advance notice of weakness in the market as a whole.

Don't mirror the Pros here by thinking that "if I invest in the larger more stable blue chips I can avoid the next large decline." Jesse Livermore said it best, "To 'buy and hold' blindly on the basis that it is a great company, or a strong industry, or the economy's general health is, to me, the equivalent of stock-market suicide." As I mentioned earlier, Mutual Funds invest in larger companies during market corrections not because they want to, but because they HAVE to. Unlike the individual investor, they are not allowed to move fully to cash, so they need to find the next best thing … the best of the worst if you will.

I see time and time again the market moving up and while the other indexes continue higher, the NASDAQ stalls and starts declining or closing flat with no gains. Then as the NASDAQ starts to actually decline, the rest of the market gets dragged down with it (after the NASDAQ). The NASDAQ doesn't *always* lead the entire market, but I am continually impressed with its ability to provide reliable clues as to the future direction of the entire market.

The beauty of all of this is that this is the only index / stock chart you ever need to look at in order to protect your investments. Using the technique in this book while looking at the NASDAQ, you will be protected from all major declines.

You can't actually trade the NASDAQ or any *index* for that matter, so you must use an ETF that mirrors the NASDAQ closely although it isn't necessary if you have a preference to invest in something different. In other words you will use the NASDAQ gauge the health of the whole market for your entry and exit signals, and then invest in something different.

Although I have tested trading S&P 500, IWM, Dow Jones ETFs as well as individual blue chip stocks all with success, I personally use the buy/sell signals from the NASDAQ and trade the QQQ ETF. QQQ consists of the 100 largest non-financial stocks in the Nasdaq Composite. Since I prefer to mirror as closely as I can, the index that I am monitoring, QQQ is about as close as you can get to the NASDAQ.

With that said, please feel free to trade something different if you prefer. Remember, the primary goal of our analysis is to understand the health of the market at any one point in time, and since three out of four stocks tend to move in the same direction of the market, trading in something different, generally is ok.

One argument for trading QQQ is that it is one of the most widely traded ETFs in the world and with volume comes stability in price. You don't get wild swings on a daily basis (especially in after-hours trading) that you would get from a smaller ETF or individual stock … and stability is what I look for when trading the markets. You can trade your 401k, IRAs, Trust, SEP-IRA and all regular taxable accounts without restriction in QQQ.

One argument against using QQQ is its' heavy weighting of its' top 10 stocks. When you buy one hundred dollars worth of QQQ, you are NOT getting an equal share of 100 companies …

$1.00 doesn't get invested equally in each of the 100 companies, but rather … as with the NASDAQ, they weight the ETF based on the market cap of the companies. What this ultimately means is that you will own a larger share of the large companies and a smaller share of the smallest companies. In some ways this is good since the larger companies are going to be more stable but the unequal weighting can drag on the performance of the ETF. In fact in late 2012, both the NASDAQ and QQQ were pulled down because Apple's stock had a difficult last two quarters and performance was affected as a result.

At the time of this writing, the top 5 holdings in QQQ make up over 35% of the allocation. This means that if you invested $100.00, 35.00 would be invested in only 5 companies, albeit the largest in the index. In this case, 12% Apple, 8% Microsoft, 7% Google, 4% Amazon and 3% Intel. Some might consider this heavy weighting a bonus, but you just need to be aware of the ramifications if you choose to invest with such a small exposure.

In terms of sector distribution in QQQ, over 50% is technology based, so again … just something to be aware of. Sometimes this strong focus will help your portfolio and other times it will hinder it.

Chapter 20

How to Read a Stock Chart

For those of you that have never seen a stock chart, the next two chapters are for you. If you are familiar with stock charts and moving averages, you can skip these.

When looking at a stock chart, you generally see one of two types. One is called an 'OHLC' or Open, High, Low, Close chart and the second is a 'Candlestick' chart; they both show the same information. Each icon or 'candlestick' on a chart represents one period in time. From the candlestick, you can identify the opening price for the period of time, as well as the highest, lowest and closing prices.

As an example, if you are looking at an annual chart, each single candlestick would represent one year of time, and the open would be the opening price on the very first trading day of January, while the high and low would show you the highest and lowest price that was achieved throughout that year, and of course, the close would represent the very last price of the year in late December.

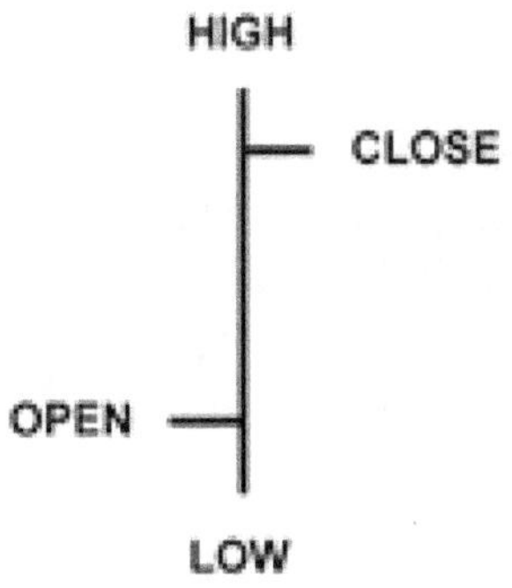

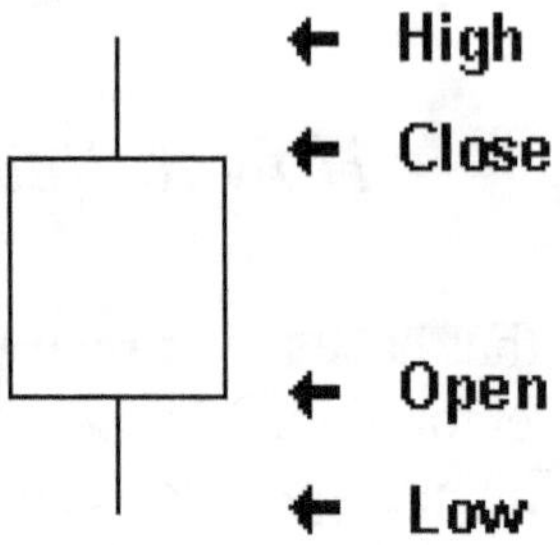

Most default charts show *daily* candlesticks and for our purposes this is what we want to look at, but just keep in mind that your charting software has the ability to change the context to minutes, hours, days, weeks, months, quarters and years and as the *period* of time changes, so does the context of what you are looking at.

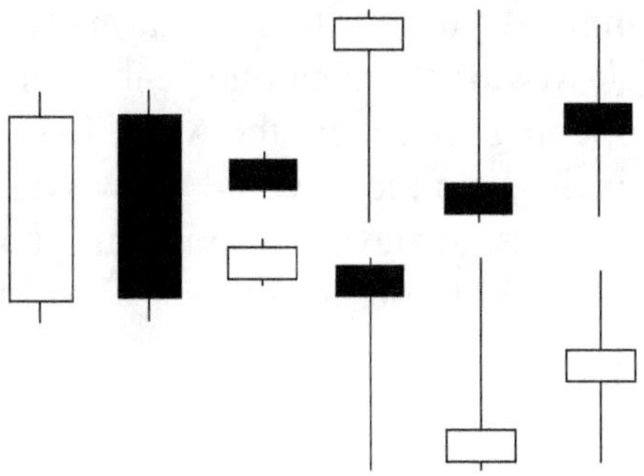

The candlesticks can sometimes look pretty funky, but we keep things really simply with the strategy and don't worry about trying to decipher their individual nuances. Just remember that if you are looking at a daily chart, each vertical red or black candlestick represents a day in the market, regardless of how the candlestick looks (red, black, full, skinny, etc).

And as you will soon see with the strategy, we only concern ourselves with the highest and lowest point of each daily candlestick, since we only care about the high and low of each day. This means that regardless of what type of chart you are looking at, we only monitor the absolute top (the highest point) and absolute bottom (the lowest point) of each candlestick.

Chapter 21

The Moving Average, the Only Indicator You Need to Know

In Technical Analysis, one of the most heavily watched indicators is the 'Moving Average' (MA). A moving average is the average closing price over a set period of time and displayed as a line going across (from left to right) a stock chart. Each point along the line represents the average price at that moment, over a set period of time, so a 20-day moving average basically shows you the average closing price over the past 20 days, a 20-week moving average shows you the average closing price over the past 20 weeks, and a 20-hour moving average would show you the average closing price over the past 20 hours of time.

Traders will use different lengths of time in their moving average calculation based on the time period they are looking to trade. The longer your time horizon (holding period), the longer the moving average, should be. In other words, using a 50-day moving average should be used for multi-month to multi-year holds, while shorter time periods will be more reactive to the current situation. Obviously looking at a 50-year moving average (showing the average closing price of the past 50 years) would not be very effective if you were a day trader looking to capitalize on the price movements of the next one to two hours.

What is interesting about the moving average in general is that it is probably the most widely used technical analysis *tool* for most traders. In fact, the big institutional players use a 50-day moving average as a buying signal and an indication on the strength of the market (or individual stock). If a stock is above the 50-day moving average it represents that this stock is being accumulated and is desirable, whereas when the price closes below the 50-day moving average, it represents that a position is being sold by the masses and might not be desirable any longer.

In our case, we will be using the 20-day moving average (20 DMA), so if I don't say otherwise, assume we are using a daily moving average. To calculate a *daily* moving average, you take the closing price of the last 20 days and add them all together, then divide that number by 20. So you take the last 20 days and add up the price they closed at on each of the 20 days, then divide by 20.

It's a really simple calculation; yet as I will show you shortly, charting software makes this even easier for you since the software will calculate these numbers for you. When working with charting software, be aware of the time period that is being displayed. Although the default value is usually daily, charting software allows you to use minutes, hours, days, weeks, months, quarters and years to calculate a moving average, so if you decide to use charting software make certain you are looking at a *daily* moving average and not something else.

Since the moving average is an average closing price of the last xx days, when prices are rising the moving average is also trending higher (the line has an upward slant), and when prices start falling they pull the moving average down with it … so as the market starts to fall into a correction you see a rising moving average become flat and then downward sloping.

A rising moving average quickly tells you that the market is rising whereas a downward sloping (declining) average means that the market is in a decline. This is the power of using a moving average as a gauge of the health of the market, you never 'buy and ~~*hold*~~ hope' while prices are falling … because as an uptrend comes to an end, prices start falling and they quickly fall below the 20-day moving average (the average price over the last 20 days) pulling the MA down with it. So watching price relative to the moving average keeps us out of a dangerous situation where we lose our capital since a major decline will push price below the moving average near the beginning of a downward move, and then drop precipitously from there.

It is important to note that a moving average includes the current day's value in its' equation, so a 20-day moving average takes the average closing price of today and the previous 19 days. If you are looking for the MA value during market hours (the stock-market closes at 4pm eastern time), you would use the current price at this moment as the closing value of today, and then add the closing price of the previous 19 days to it (then divide by 20, of course). Therefore, intraday, the value of a moving average will change slightly since we are using today's closing price in the equation and the market has yet to close. As the day's price fluctuates, one of the 20 values using to calculate the 20 DMA is changing and therefore the moving average will change (slightly) with it.

What this means for us, is that ultimately we have to wait for the market to close in order to know the 20-day moving average for that day. Therefore, we make our decision as to whether to adjust our portfolio at the end of the day. This means you can either make transactions a few minutes before the close, 'after-hours' (the market technically is open for 'after-hours trading' until 8pm eastern time), or at the open the next morning. At Resnn, we generally trade within the last 5 minutes of the trading day or after-hours.

A quick word of caution using after-hours trading, since there are fewer buyers and sellers once the market officially closes, sometimes the price is not as favorable, although usually it is a wash where sometimes you get a better price and other times worse. A bigger issue to be aware of with after-hours trading if you are buying or selling low volume (lightly traded) stocks is that you can end up paying a very steep markup since there are fewer buyers and sellers. But as we already discussed, we trade large index funds (QQQ, IWM, SPY, etc), where after-hours trading is fine to do since there is so much demand.

Chapter 22

Using Online Resources to Calculate Your Entry and Exit Points

As we already discussed, we are going to need to calculate a 20-day moving average but since I for one, do not get giddy at the thought of opening a spreadsheet and doing math every day, there are a number of websites and brokerage software that will do this automatically for us.

But first, I want to reiterate how simple the charts are that we will be using. Remember we don't need fancy software or anything expensive; we just need a basic *daily* chart that shows the highest and lowest points that were achieved during the day in relation to the moving average. A quick visual that should take no more than 20 seconds of your day. Nothing fancy.

My two favorites are www.FreeStockCharts.com and www.StockCharts.com. Both websites offer premium technical analysis tools (for a monthly fee) which are an amazing help when studying price movements, but for us the free portion provides everything we will need.

I'm particularly fond of FreeStockCharts.com because of its' ease in adding new indicators to your charts AND its' ability to remember your settings when you close your browser and come back a day later. FreeStockCharts.com has a great tutorial under the HELP menu at the top of the screen. At the time of this writing FreeStockCharts.com will not work on an iPad or iPhone, where as StockCharts.com will.

In this chapter, I will be providing a quick tutorial on how to setup the charts we need at both websites, but please know that the process I describe below might be quite different by the time you read this. Technology moves quickly, so it is quite possible that by the time you read this there will be better tools out there. Having said that, remember we don't need anything advanced to calculate what we need. In fact, you can use a calculator and paper if you are so inclined.

Let's start with FreeStockCharts.com, my favorite simply because of the amount of tools they provide (for free) at your fingertips. When you first get to their home page, it automatically loads a stock's (or index) chart. To change to a different stock or index (called a symbol), select from the FILE menu "Search for Symbol/Company."

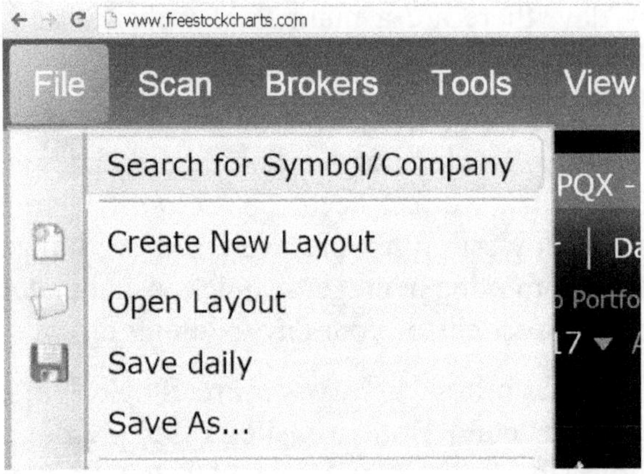

When you select that, a pop up window appears allowing you to enter a company name or stock index. In our case, we want to use the NASDAQ, so … type in the word NASDAQ and you will see a list of choices.

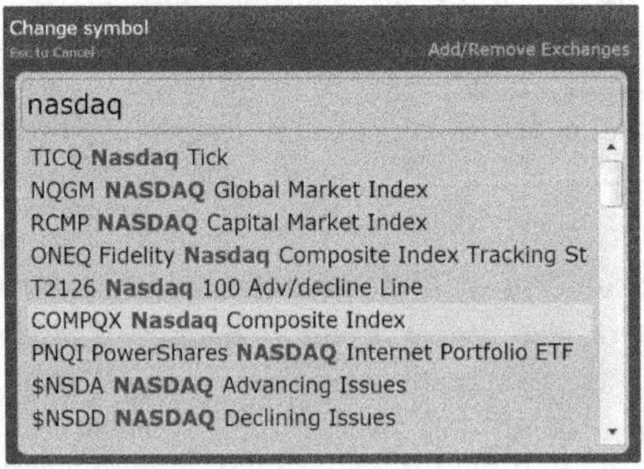

Select the "Nasdaq Composite Index" from the pull down and the chart will refresh showing you the NASDAQ. Notice at the top left of the screen it shows the symbol we selected (in this case the NASDAQ's symbol which is COMPQX), and the time period that you are viewing, which is most likely *daily.* If you don't see daily, but rather see the word "hourly", "weekly", "monthly", "quarterly" or "yearly", click on the word to change it to "daily".

Now, you need to add the Moving Average 'indicator.' Click the "ADD INDICATOR" button at the very left top of the chart and select "MOVING AVERAGE" from the available list of indicators. This will automatically add a 50-day moving average 'line' to the chart.

Let's now change the moving average period of time from a 50-day to a 20-day. Click on the indicator at the very top (see screenshot above) and select "edit" to open the "edit moving average" window, where you can change the time "Period" from 50 to 20 and click ok. This will change the chart instantly to show a 20-day moving average. FYI, you do not need to adjust any other settings on the moving average option window.

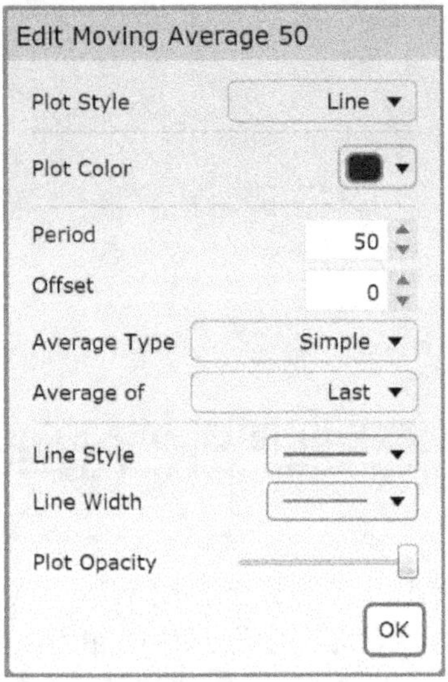

And with that, you are done customizing the chart; this is all that is needed to be setup for our analysis. Remember also that the next time you return to FreeStockCharts.com, your settings will be remembered, so you only have to do the above one time and all future days involve just loading the page and quickly looking to see the price relative to the moving average.

By the way, on FreeStockCharts.com, if you roll your mouse over the chart, a pop-up shows the pricing information for a specific day, so it becomes really easy to see how the close is relative to the moving average.

Now let's go over to StockCharts.com to see how you setup a chart there. At the home page, look for the blue box on the far right of the screen that is labeled "Start to Chart!"

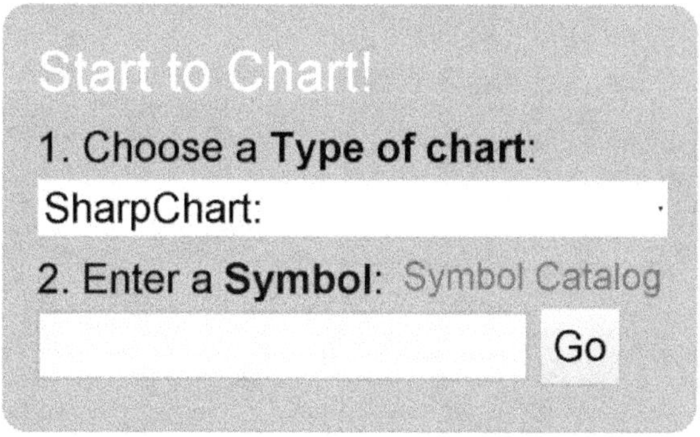

Then select "Sharpchart:" as the type of chart, and type in NASDAQ in the symbol box and click GO. The page will refresh with a daily chart of the NASDAQ with all sorts of indicators overlaid on the chart. Below the chart is the preference section allowing you to add or remove indicators, including showing longer time periods and changing the type of chart.

Remember the only indicator we care about is the 20-day moving average, so below the chart in the overlay section, change one of the moving averages to 20 and remove all others … and click update to show the changes in the chart above.

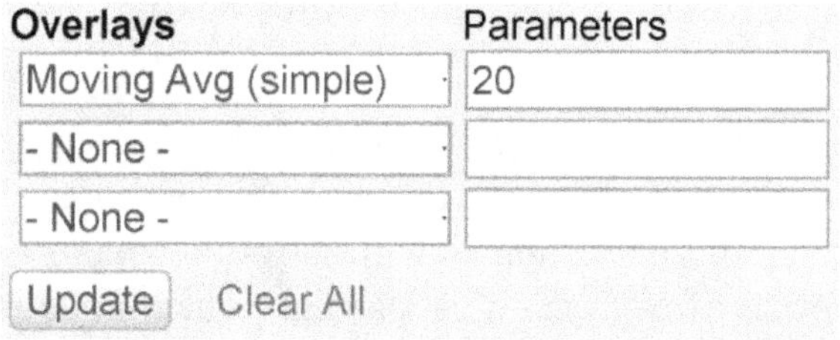

After you click the update button, it should look something like the chart below. Remember if yours has a lot of other indicators on it, you can remove them below the chart, but you don't need to if you don't want.

Notice in the chart above, at the top left, I underlined the MA20. On your own chart, make sure you see this to know you setup the moving average correctly with 20 periods. Also, notice slightly above this, you will see the word "daily", indicating to us that each candlestick on the chart represents one day and therefore the moving average we are looking is based on daily values as well.

One important note, at the top of the screen you will notice an "inspect" check box. If you click this, you can then roll your mouse over the chart and it will show the open, high, low and closing price of each candlestick that your mouse is rolled over. This is helpful to analyze days in the past where the price gets really close to the moving average but you can't tell visually whether it has actually touched the moving average or not.

Chapter 23

The Magic Formula

HOW TO CONSISTENTLY OUTPERFORM THE MARKET

Hopefully by now, you have a clear understanding of how to read a stock chart and how to add a moving average to the chart. If you are a bit confused, don't worry, this is new territory for most. You might try rereading the previous two chapters OR it might become clear shortly as you see examples below. Just remember that if you are looking at a daily chart, each vertical red or black candlestick represents a day in the market, and that we only concern ourselves with the highest and lowest point of each daily candlestick and how that point is in relation to the moving average. Everything else on the chart is not relevant to our discussion so don't let a bunch of clutter confuse you.

I will give examples in a moment, but first I want to give you the specific entry and exit signals that we will use. Remember the entire system is designed to take 1 minute-each-week, only 20 seconds-a-day. In fact, most weeks will never involve a trade, you will be in the market already and stay invested, or out of the market with no change required. But regardless of no trades occurring, what is required each week is to monitor the market for changes that may result in loss.

> ***"True professional traders do not concern themselves with why things have happened; rather, they simply accept change as an unavoidable part of trading and adapt to current conditions."*** *- David Baker*

We don't trade just to trade, but we also don't 'buy and ~~*hold*~~ hope;' when the trend changes we change our behavior as well to match the markets sentiment … either aggressive (in the market) or protective (out of the market).

> ***"There is only one side of the market and it is not the bull side or the bear side, but the right side."*** *– Jesse Livermore*

ENTRY SIGNAL

ENTER THE MARKET WHEN THE LOW OF THE NASDAQ REMAINS ABOVE THE 20-DAY MOVING AVERAGE FOR THREE CONSECUTIVE DAYS. WHEN YOU ENTER THE MARKET, YOU GO FULLY IN … INVESTING 100% OF YOUR PORTFOLIO, AND YOU STAY IN UNTIL YOU RECEIVE AN EXIT SIGNAL.

EXIT SIGNAL

EXIT THE MARKET WHEN THE HIGH OF THE NASDAQ REMAINS BELOW THE 20-DAY MOVING AVERAGE FOR THREE CONSECUTIVE DAYS. EXITING MEANS GOING FULLY TO CASH AND STAYING OUT OF THE MARKET UNTIL YOU RECEIVE A NEW ENTRY SIGNAL

Chapter 24

Anatomy of a Trade

In a moment I will explain the *why* … why this simple technique works so well, but first let's walk through a typical trade using the 20-day moving average so you can see the above in action. Notice the stock chart below (from StockCharts.com). These are the actual trades that we made in late 2012 through the second quarter of 2013. I have marked five points on the chart below.

Just to recap our trading signals, you enter the market fully (100% in) when the NASDAQ's low (of the day) stays above the 20-day moving average for three consecutive days, and exit completely (100% in cash) when the NASDAQ's high (of the day) remains below the 20-day moving average for three consecutive days.

We actually entered the market at Point B on 11/27/2012 and exited at Point E (4/8/2013) resulting in an 8.6% gain for the period.

But first, Point A shows when we exited from the previous trade. As you can see we avoided a substantial decline after our exit. Look at day 1 in the chart below showing a zoomed in view of point A, notice how on 10/8/2013, the market gapped down at the open under the 20-day moving average (the line on the chart) and closed well under. Following our rules, this is day one where the NASDAQ's highest price of the day remained under the 20 DMA. Remember in order to exit the market, the NASDAQ's high must never be above the moving average for three consecutive days. The next two days continued the downward path (marked on the chart below as days 2 and 3). As you can see, the price never got close to touching the 20-day moving average during these three days and so at the end of the 3rd day we exited.

The next few days the market bounced (up), as is usual after a multi-day decline, but you can see the bounce was short lived. In fact, the 20 DMA acted as a barrier that price was not able to climb above, which is typical. Our exit point proved to be prudent.

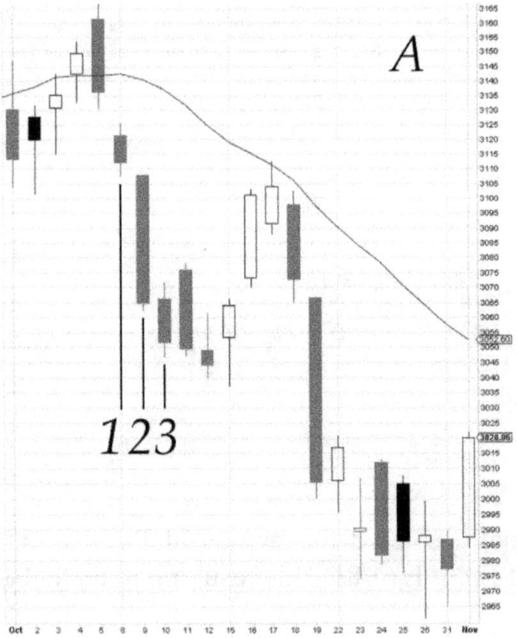

Now let's look at our entry (point B)

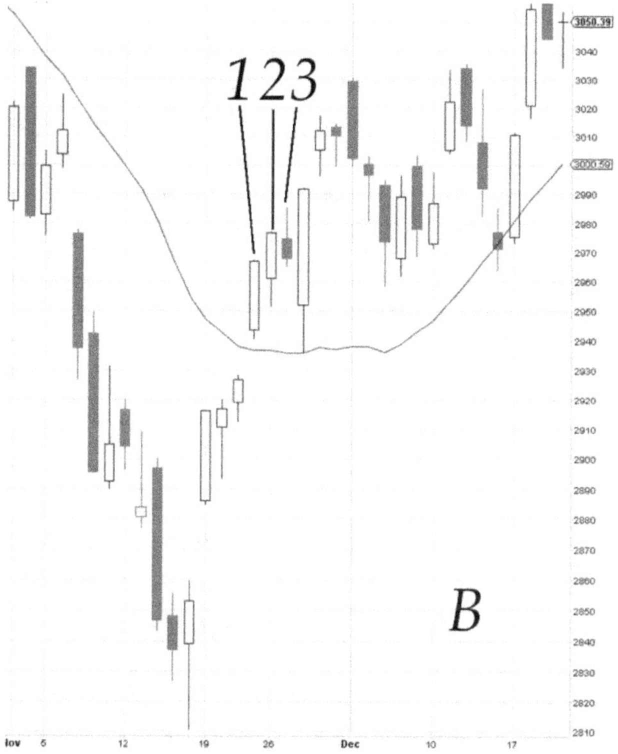

Point B – after a strong decline from September, 2012, the market finally stabilized in November, 2013.

Remember that when we are out of the market, in order to get back in, we look for three days in a row where the low remains above (never touches or crosses) the moving average; this shows us that there is strength in the market and acts as our buy signal. You can see from the large chart at the start of this chapter that prior to our entry in late November (between points A and B), there were a number of days in mid October to early November where the NASDAQ got close to the moving average but it was not able to get above it. This showed us that there was still further weakness in store for the market. If the Institutional 'players' don't have enough conviction to push price above the MA, then we also should have no conviction and stay defensive.

On November 23rd (point B) the market gapped up at the open and closed above the 20-day moving average for the first time in almost 2 months. The low of the day was above the moving average, so we count this as the first day. Two more days like this and we will enter the market. Notice on day 2 and day 3, we continued to stay above the moving average (the low of the day never crossed the 20 DMA) and as a result this was our signal to enter the market. So, we enter here and wait … after this we don't do much except monitor the situation looking for a change in behavior.

Note that on the third day, the market actually closed with a loss, a *down* day, but this doesn't affect our decision to enter. All we care about is that the low of the day never fell below the moving average.

> ***"I knew I could not predict anything and that is why we decided to follow trends. No matter how ridiculous those trends appear to be at the beginning, and no matter how extended or how irrational they seem at the end, we simply follow trends. And that is why we've been so successful."*** *- John Henry*

As long as the price remains above the moving average, we just sit on our hands and enjoy the rising market. Each day we need to look at the chart once and if it is still above the MA, we are done with our analysis for the day. No more than 20 seconds of time! It is not until the price moves below the moving average that we need to take a closer look, which occurred at Point C.

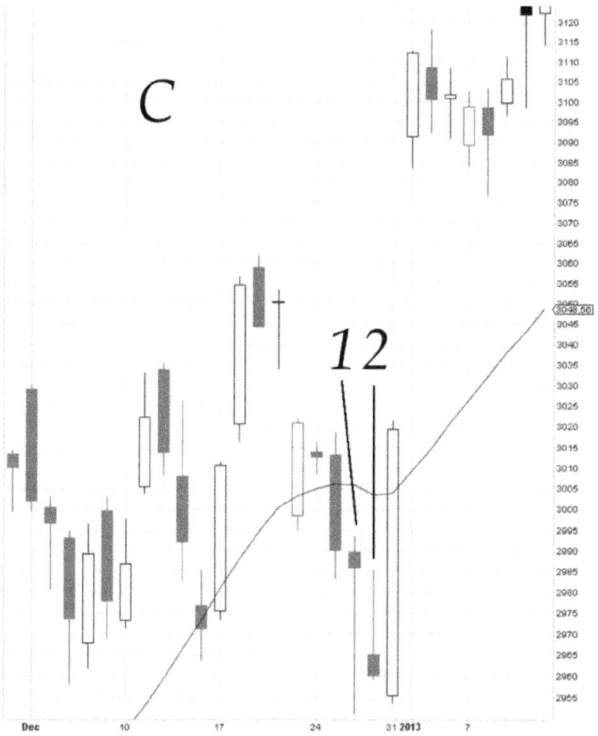

Looking at point C closer, we see that in late December, the price pierced below the moving average and closed below it. The next day, December 27th, 2012 the high never was able to get above the moving average, so we count this as day one in our 3-day count. Two more days where the high does not cross (or touch) the moving average and we will exit.

Day 2 continues the downward trend and gets counted, but on the third day we have a strong up day and we actually close above the moving average. It doesn't matter where the close is for the day only that the high of the day was able to get above the moving average (even if only for a few minutes during the day), which it did … resetting our 3-day count back to zero.

This was a scary 'shake-out,' but because of our rules we stayed fully invested without feeling any pain. Remember … following your rules is imperative for long-term success in the market.

Roughly 2 months later, in late February we have another small correction (at point D). Of course, we don't know it will be small while it is happening, so we need to always assume the worst case and follow our rules; always protecting ourselves, just in case. On February 20th, the NASDAQ closed below the moving average for the first time in the year, and so we need to start watching more closely. The next day, February 21st (point 1 in chart D above), the high of the day stayed below the moving average, so this counts as day one in our 3-day count. The next day, the same thing occurred … this becomes day two of our 3-day count, one more day where the high remains below the MA and we exit.

But, on day three, sure enough … the high of the day pierced the moving average which reset our count back to zero. Notice that we closed severely below the moving average for the day, but all we are concerned with is if the high *broke* the moving average or not, and it did. The fact that we were able to pierce the MA intraday is a small sign of strength that the buyers are still interested in the market.

With the count reset, we now need three new days where the high stays below (not crossing or touching) the moving average. And sure enough on the fourth day, the high of the day does indeed remain below the MA … this becomes day one in our 3-day count. But on the fifth day, the high crosses above the moving average again and so once again we reset our count. Day six, seven and eight all pierce the moving average (the high is above the MA each day), so we just stay invested and keep watching with a count of zero. Finally on day nine, we get a strong bounce which fortunately keeps the trend alive and us in the market, weathering another small correction with no pain. Follow your rules!!

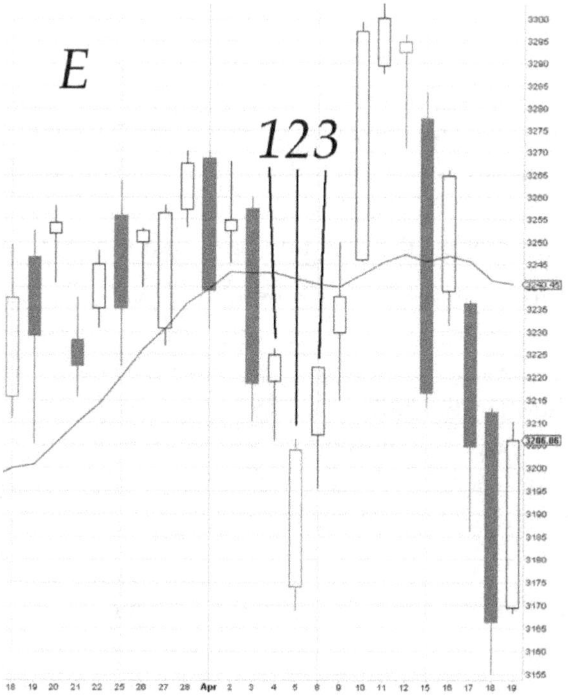

The market proceeded up for a few more months, and then on April 3rd (point E) we again closed below the 20 DMA. The next day, April 4th, the high of the day stayed below the MA making this the first day in our 3-day count. The next day also remained below the 20 DMA raising our count to two. All we need now is one more day where the high remains below the MA to exit the market. And sure enough on the third day, we again remained below the MA, finally we have three days where the high remained below the moving average; time to exit the market. In this case, we were in the market for a total of 89 trading days (from November until April) and gained 8.6%.

> ***"Being in the markets with rules is the only way to trade"*** *- Michael Covel*

From here, we start looking for a point to re-enter the market by looking for three straight days where the low of the day stays above the moving average. Sometimes this happens almost immediately as in this case, but other times we may be out for many months. **The point is we let the market's health and our rules dictate whether we re-enter. It doesn't matter what's going on in the news or what we *think* the market is going to do; all that matters is what actually happens with the price.** If the market drops, we are protected, but if the market stabilizes and continues higher, then we hop back in and ride it up again.

Hopefully you can see from the above example, that the process is very straight forward and simple. Three consecutive days where the low stays above the 20-day moving average and we enter the market until we have 3 consecutive days where the high stays below the moving average and we exit. That's it, roughly 5-10 seconds of analysis a day, then every once in awhile we need to login to our brokerage account and buy or sell.

Let's now change our focus to understanding *why* a 3-day moving average strategy is so effective at keeping you safe.

Chapter 25

Why the Strategy Works

WHY ARE THREE DAYS SIGNIFICANT?

The three-day cycle is actually fairly well known in day-trading circles, but not for longer-term trend traders. The premise behind the three-day rule is that on day one the institutional investors buy (or sell) a large amount of stock causing a dramatic change in the existing trend. Then, on day 2, after seeing such a dramatic move the day prior, the retail 'do-it-yourself' investors follow suit. These guys are notorious for chasing performance, usually without a plan or rules and mostly underperform as a result. They see a big move in a stock and want to be a part of it. Then on the third day we usually see a reversal where the institutional guys on the first day reverse their orders, exiting and taking advantage of the dumb money that got in on day 2. It is a traditional shake-out and a regular occurrence in the market.

So the premise here is that if a change in the market's direction can survive past three days ... it is likely that it will continue. This is particularly true in larger market indexes and ETFs which are much harder to manipulate as an individual stock. If a major index like the NASDAQ has a change in direction and is able to hold that change for 3 days ... we likely have a new direction in front of us. Two days isn't enough time to prove the trend is going to survive and four days causes you to enter too late resulting in worse performance over time.

WHY THE 20-DAY MOVING AVERAGE? AND, WHY NOT USE A DIFFERENT MOVING AVERAGE?

Moving averages are heavily used by active investors; in fact, you will notice that most charting programs put a moving average on their charts by default. The 20-day and 50-day moving averages in particular are the most widely watched and represent a huge psychological level for both short-term and long-term traders. If a stock cannot hold its' 20 DMA, then it is likely that significant weakness is in store in the near future … and in our case we only give the market 3 days to change its' mind and move higher before we take the cautious road and exit.

CAN YOU USE A DIFFERENT MOVING AVERAGE?

Yes, in fact, using almost any moving average provides a better return than a 'buy and hold.' Both the 20 and 50 DMA's more than double a 'buy and ~~hold~~ hope' strategy. Ironically over the past 40 years, the 50-day returns the most over time (see appendix for specifics), but it does so with larger declines in the bad years.

We use 20 days, since it provides a good middle ground. When a stock is not able to stay above the 20-day moving average, it shows there is a problem and further weakness is likely. I have found the 20-day is most effective in missing larger declines, while not taking you out of the market constantly for small insignificant drops. Remember, missing the large declines is ultimately what keeps you outperforming the average investor.

Whichever moving average you ultimately decide to follow, the trading signals are no different, we simply watch price relative to the moving average and if the low stays above the MA for 3 days we enter, and if the high stays below the MA for three days we exit.

SO, WHY WATCH SOMETHING THAT EVERYONE ELSE WATCHES? ISN'T THAT THE WORST THING TO DO?

The mere fact that the moving average is so widely used is important in itself. If everyone sees the price of a stock or index close below a moving average and they associate this close as a bearish (bad) situation, what are they going to do? They are going to sell their position.

> ***"If you argue with the market, you will lose"*** – *Larry Hite*

In fact, this *bad* association is important to note … many times the markets creates self-fulfilling prophecies, and this is one example. The idea goes like this, all traders know that stocks trading under a moving average is generally bearish for that stock, so when it closes below the moving average they all sell, causing the stock to decline and therefore confirming their original analysis … self fulfilling. Mathematicians call this a 'causal loop.'

Remember, the market is all about human behavior and moves in the market are caused by emotional reactions to events. This is why the market drops much quicker than it rises … once panic sets in, people react very quickly since fear is a stronger emotion than greed.

Moving averages are even used heavily by the less emotional players as they provide major sell and buy points for institutional traders … and let's face it … should you follow the behavior of someone that has billions of dollars to invest and can potentially move the market with their buying patterns or should you mirror a friend of yours' (who has a few hundred thousand or even a few million) because his son-in-law heard there's a new company with a supposedly great product that will revolutionize their industry.

A funny, yet sad, 'bummer man' story … my uncle worked with Bill Gates' father and was actually asked if he wanted to "get in on the ground floor" of his son's startup. He was told that his son was starting a software company and that it would be *the next big thing*. This was obviously before Microsoft was a household name. Unfortunately like what I suggest above, my uncle passed on the *opportunity*. OMG … could you imagine how different my uncle's life would have been if he invested in the company in its' early days??

I am an Angel Investor myself and therefore work with startup companies trying to secure funding quite often; the reality is that my uncle's potential outcome is a rare story.

Most early stage investments like the opportunity he had end up going belly up, so without having hindsight … my uncle probably did the right thing. Here's the reality … if you want to take some play money that you will never miss if it is lost and invest in a handful of startups, I have no issue with it, but don't gamble your entire portfolio … there is just too much at stake to operate this way.

Bottom line, we use the KISS principle. Don't over think the strategy, it is designed to be simple and it works. The rules are straightforward, but they *must* be followed to have the desired outcome. If you feel really bullish and stay in the market when an exit signal triggers, you do so at your own risk. The strategy took years of research to discover and perfect, and straying from it will most likely have poor results. I do not use 10-day moving average or the 100-day moving average, because I have researched the optimum MA's to use. I do not suggest exiting after two days or four days, but rather three … because that is the optimum amount of time. Keep it simple, but at the same time do it correctly.

Chapter 26

A Word of Caution

As I mentioned previously, there will be times where the market can't make up its' mind and you get 'whip-sawed,' buying at the top then watching the price fall below the moving average and ultimately causing an exit signal, only after to see the market stabilize and move higher.

Although these times are quite frustrating, the important thing to remember is that although they do occur, they aren't in the majority. You will notice in the list of all trades over the past 41 years (included in the appendix), that there are a number of times where these whip-saws occur, but since we only give the market three days to make up its' mind, your loss each time is minimal.

> ***"If a speculator is correct half of the time, he is hitting a good average. Even being right 3 or 4 times out of 10 should yield a fortune if he has the sense to cut his losses quickly on the ventures where he has been wrong."*** – *Bernard Baruch*

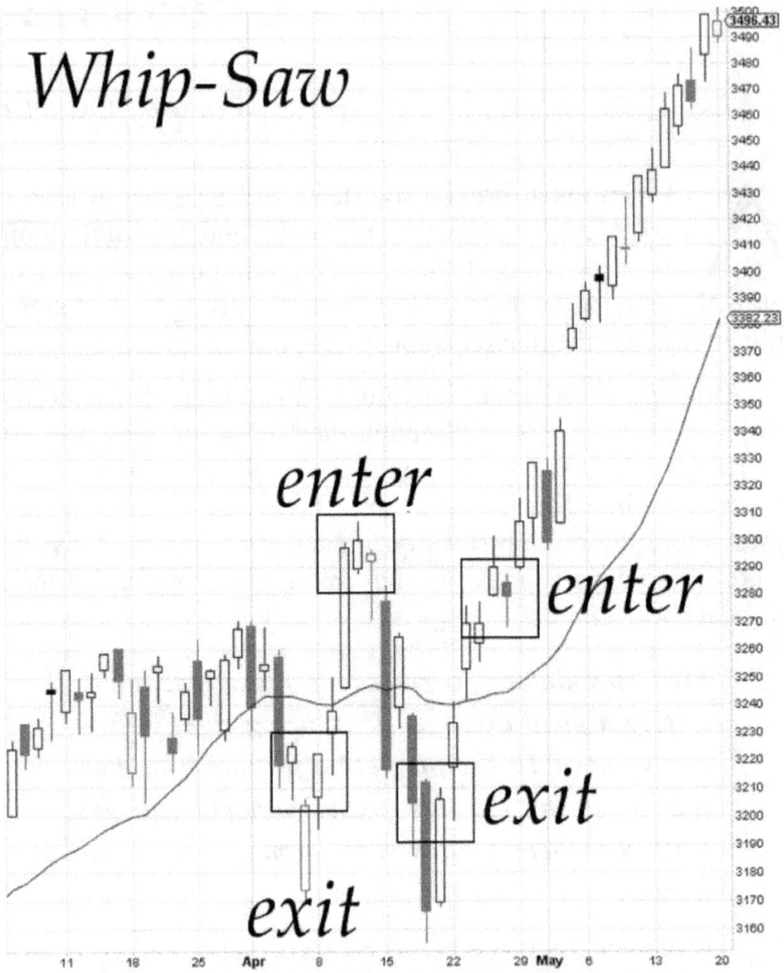

Whipsaw ... A classic Buy High and Sell Low strategy,

Not the best way to make money!!

Remember the strategy has roughly a 50% win rate … so there are definitely times where these losing trades occur. Although the whipsaws are hard to sit through, you have to remember that these times are few and over the long haul it clearly works out to your favor. Remember, that the strategy allows us to lose up to 4 times in a row and still make money.

Chapter 27

The Performance

On the next page is a side by side annual comparison of the strategy with the NASDAQ. Sure you would've made more money using one of the strategies in this book over a 'buy and hold,' but at what expense? How much pain do you have to feel in order to end up better in the end? In other words, I would not be willing to risk a 90% loss in order to get a 150% gain. The risk is just too high for me.

This chart helps to get a gauge of that worst-case scenario. I encourage you not to just look at the bottom line, but rather do what the Pros do and look at each and every year to get a feel for the strategy.

I have also included in the appendix a list of every trade made along with the win/loss ratios. That coupled with this chart should help you to gain an expectation of the strategy. I encourage you to run your own analysis to verify the results for yourself. **Remember to 'Trust, but Verify.'**

All strategies started with $10,000.00 on 1/1/1973 and ended on 12/31/2013, 41 years later.

20-DAY MOVING AVERAGE

Ending Value: $919,152.00

Cumulative Return: 9,091.5%

Average Annual Return (IRR): 11.66%

Largest 1 year decline: -13.1%

Vs.

NASDAQ 'BUY AND HOLD'

Ending Value: $408,296.00

Cumulative Return: 3,983.0%

Average Annual Return (IRR): 9.47%

Largest 1 year decline: -40.5%

Year	20 Day Moving Average			NASDAQ		
	start	end	+/-	start	end	+/-
1973	$ 10,000	$ 10,344	3.4%	$ 10,000	$ 8,655	-13.5%
1974	$ 10,344	$ 8,986	-13.1%	$ 8,655	$ 5,616	-35.1%
1975	$ 8,986	$ 11,268	25.4%	$ 5,616	$ 7,287	29.8%
1976	$ 11,268	$ 12,685	12.6%	$ 7,287	$ 9,189	26.1%
1977	$ 12,685	$ 12,420	-2.1%	$ 9,189	$ 9,862	7.3%
1978	$ 12,420	$ 13,518	8.8%	$ 9,862	$ 11,076	12.3%
1979	$ 13,518	$ 16,304	20.6%	$ 11,076	$ 14,189	28.1%
1980	$ 16,304	$ 22,455	37.7%	$ 14,189	$ 18,995	33.9%
1981	$ 22,455	$ 24,813	10.5%	$ 18,995	$ 18,385	-3.2%
1982	$ 24,813	$ 32,518	31.1%	$ 18,385	$ 21,818	18.7%
1983	$ 32,518	$ 39,947	22.8%	$ 21,818	$ 26,155	19.9%
1984	$ 39,947	$ 36,009	-9.9%	$ 26,155	$ 23,221	-11.2%
1985	$ 36,009	$ 46,840	30.1%	$ 23,221	$ 30,504	31.4%
1986	$ 46,840	$ 51,878	10.8%	$ 30,504	$ 32,748	7.4%
1987	$ 51,878	$ 59,279	14.3%	$ 32,748	$ 31,024	-5.3%
1988	$ 59,279	$ 65,713	10.9%	$ 31,024	$ 35,804	15.4%
1989	$ 65,713	$ 73,156	11.3%	$ 35,804	$ 42,698	19.3%
1990	$ 73,156	$ 77,987	6.6%	$ 42,698	$ 35,096	-17.8%
1991	$ 77,987	$ 103,244	32.4%	$ 35,096	$ 55,045	56.8%
1992	$ 103,244	$ 116,079	12.4%	$ 55,045	$ 63,551	15.5%
1993	$ 116,079	$ 132,346	14.0%	$ 63,551	$ 72,925	14.8%
1994	$ 132,346	$ 122,178	-7.7%	$ 72,925	$ 70,593	-3.2%
1995	$ 122,178	$ 156,962	28.5%	$ 70,593	$ 98,773	39.9%
1996	$ 156,962	$ 203,231	29.5%	$ 98,773	$ 121,201	22.7%
1997	$ 203,231	$ 232,123	14.2%	$ 121,201	$ 147,423	21.6%
1998	$ 232,123	$ 315,603	36.0%	$ 147,423	$ 205,848	39.6%
1999	$ 315,603	$ 440,512	39.6%	$ 205,848	$ 382,023	85.6%
2000	$ 440,512	$ 400,051	-9.2%	$ 382,023	$ 231,930	-39.3%
2001	$ 400,051	$ 426,079	6.5%	$ 231,930	$ 183,102	-21.1%
2002	$ 426,079	$ 392,549	-7.9%	$ 183,102	$ 125,376	-31.5%
2003	$ 392,549	$ 479,180	22.1%	$ 125,376	$ 188,065	50.0%
2004	$ 479,180	$ 541,166	12.9%	$ 188,065	$ 204,228	8.6%
2005	$ 541,166	$ 543,093	0.4%	$ 204,228	$ 207,033	1.4%
2006	$ 543,093	$ 541,101	-0.4%	$ 207,033	$ 226,745	9.5%
2007	$ 541,101	$ 503,686	-6.9%	$ 226,745	$ 248,994	9.8%
2008	$ 503,686	$ 480,846	-4.5%	$ 248,994	$ 148,050	-40.5%
2009	$ 480,846	$ 590,512	22.8%	$ 148,050	$ 213,026	43.9%
2010	$ 590,512	$ 656,694	11.2%	$ 213,026	$ 249,049	16.9%
2011	$ 656,694	$ 626,335	-4.6%	$ 249,049	$ 244,569	-1.8%
2012	$ 626,335	$ 725,575	15.8%	$ 244,569	$ 283,469	15.9%
2013	$ 725,575	$ 919,152	26.7%	$ 283,469	$ 408,296	44.0%

Chapter 28

General Observations

Some general observations about the strategy that you may have noticed on your own...

SOMETIMES YOU WILL SELL HIGH AND BUY HIGHER, OR WORSE, BUY HIGH AND SELL LOW ...

I'm not going to sit here and tell you that I have found the Holy Grail of investing, because I haven't. But what I have found is a way to more than double the return of the NASDAQ consistently over time. Remember the main focus of the strategy is to keep you safe from major declines, and secondly to grow your investment over time. But like any investment strategy, there are periods of time where it underperforms alternatives. You need to be prepared for those times and be willing to sit through them. Remember you can have 4 losing trades in a row and still end up profitable. I have provided performance comparisons in the previous chapter so that you can see historically how we outperform some years, and underperform in others.

WHEN THE MARKET IS REALLY MOVING UP AGGRESSIVELY, THERE IS NO BETTER INVESTMENT THAN A 'BUY AND HOLD' STRATEGY

Therefore we and any other non 'buy and hold' strategy will underperform in these times. This kind of makes sense, if the market is just going up … you want to be invested during the entire rise. Granted nobody knows ahead of time what the outcome will be and whether the next decline will be just a small blip or something that takes five to fifteen years to recover from. So, although there will be times when a defensively focused strategy will underperform, obviously when the market is falling, you want to be protecting yourself and being out of the market is the only true protection during substantial declines.

THE TREND IS YOUR FRIEND

Ever heard this saying? It means that you shouldn't fight the direction of the market. If it is clearly in an uptrend you don't short the market betting it will go down, and when declining you don't invest until the market has changed direction definitively. You "don't fight the tape."

Notice in the results, the time when the market is trending (going in one direction for a long time) is when we make the *real* money, and using a moving average helps us to easily identify *the trend.* When the market is going up we enjoy the ride, but when it is not we don't sit around idly hoping that things will get better, we protect ourselves.

> ***"Throughout all my years of investing I've found that the big money was never made in the buying or the selling. The big money was made in the waiting."*** *- Jesse Livermore*

BECAUSE WE ARE WAITING FOR SIGNS OF STRENGTH BEFORE WE RISK OUR INVESTMENT, WE WILL NEVER BUY AT THE ABSOLUTE BOTTOM OR SELL AT THE ABSOLUTE TOP.

We want definitive proof that the market has changed character after a decline … before we take undo risk. We want to be certain that things have changed and that further downside is not likely.

> ***"You'll never sell at the exact top, so don't kick yourself if a stock goes higher after you sell. If you don't sell early, you'll be late. The object is to make and take significant gains and not get excited, optimistic, or greedy as a stock's advance gets stronger. Keep in mind the old saying: 'Bulls make money and bears make money, but pigs get slaughtered.' The basic***

> ***objective of every account should be to show a net profit."*** - *Bernard Baruch*

THE MAGIC FORMULA ... THERE IS NOTHING MAGICAL ABOUT IT!

In fact it is quite boring ... but the best strategies usually are. Alexander Elder said it best, "The secret to trading is that there is no secret" It isn't designed to be exciting or sexy; it is designed to keep your money safe and outperform over time. In the early years I spent a lot of time *tinkering* with our strategy at Resnn, and almost always would end up throwing away our tests because they would take away the reliability and consistent performance of our original strategy. This was a hard thing for me to embrace ... I would always say ... "if *this* is good, then adding *that* must make it better," but keeping things simple always performed more consistently. I want to repeat this important lesson, since this will save you years of wasted effort and lost opportunity. **KEEP IT SIMPLE!**

This is why most professional advisors perform no better than someone that spends no more than 1 minute-a-week investing. Unlike most industries, having more knowledge of the stock market doesn't equate to better performance. It's a hard concept to grasp, but I certainly have seen this time and time again. Keep it simple, follow your rules and you will do great!

> ***"You don't need to be a rocket scientist. Investing is not a game where the guy with the 160 IQ beats the guy with a 130 IQ. Rationality is essential."*** - *Warren Buffett*

DON'T WORRY ABOUT WIN/LOSS RATIO'S

If the market is going up, you will be going with it, and if it is goes down, you will be protected. Who cares if you have nine losses to one win, as long as that one outperforms the nine ... who cares. Remember, it really doesn't matter if you are right, only that you make money.

> ***"It is not a matter of winning every trade that is important. Net profitability after a series of trades is the key to market success."*** - *Michael Covel*

Looking at our year-to-date performance numbers in the performance chapter and comparing them to the Nasdaq, you will see we underperformed (sometimes severely) in 2003, 2009 and 1999, yet even with these severely underperforming years the strategy still blows the doors off a 'buy and ~~*hold*~~ hope' strategy over the long haul. Why? Because we miss the dramatic drops that occur consistently every few years.

Remember long-term success in the market is not determined by how well you do in the good years, but rather how less bad you do in the bad years. Capital preservation is the name of the game. So, again, don't get too fixated on short-term performance numbers, the strategy will outperform over time and protect you when you need it.

> ***"The whole secret to winning big in the stock market is not to be right all the time, but to lose the least amount possible when you're wrong."*** - *William J. O'Neil*

Chapter 29

Deep Dive

"Know what you own and know why you own it." *– Peter Lynch*

UNDERSTANDING WHY A MOVING AVERAGE STRATEGY KEEPS YOU PROTECTED

Remember earlier in the book I said things like "*Trust, but Verify*" and "*Be the captain of your own ship,*" etc. I don't want you to take my word for it that trading based off of a moving average works … I want you to know the system works, because you have verified it and understand the concepts. As you know, I have provided the actual trades over the past 41 years, so you can pull up past charts and verify for yourself … but it is important that you understand the logic behind the strategy. In other words, I've told you HOW it works, but I want to make certain you understand WHY it works. Maybe it's the way my brain works, but I personally cannot take something at face value, I need to verify that something works for me, and I want you to do the same here.

Let's discuss the moving average (for this explanation we will use the 20-day moving average) in more detail. As you know, the moving average shows the average closing price over the past 20 sessions (including today). So today's price will affect the average. Now, think about what happens if the market has big positive day today, to calculate the MA you take today's price and add it to the previous 19, then divide by 20. So if there is a big up day in the market, the MA will be higher than it was yesterday. Since we graph the MA as a line on a chart, you can imagine how an up day would raise the right side of the line causing it to be upward sloping in the near term. Conversely, if we have a big down day the moving average will be lower than it

was yesterday and as a result the line will have a downward slope.

Taking this to a chart, you will see a rising moving average (the line) when price is rising, and a declining line when price is falling. The price in a sense *leads* the average up or down, so first there is a price change and the average *follows* in the same direction.

Look closely at the chart above and watch what happens as the price changes direction from rising to falling (point 1) … you first see price start getting closer to the moving average as the MA starts *catching up* to the price, then if the weakness continues, the price crosses below the MA, which then pulls the MA down with it (point 2).

So, as long as price continues rising, the MA will *never* catch up, it will always be below it, chasing it. If the price slows down its upward path but continues to rise, the moving average will also slow down its' path and the line will be less vertical (point 3), but again the price will never touch the moving average as long as the price keeps rising. The price will only cross the moving average if we start having continued weakness.

Although 2013 wasn't a normal market since price pretty much kept rising all year without any major corrections, it provided a good way to see how the price pulls the moving average. Notice in the chart above as we see weakness in price (between points 1 and 2), the MA starts to flatten out, and as the price keeps falling, eventually the moving average starts to point downward … chasing price as it falls.

Now, let's look at our strategy in relation to the moving average. Because the moving average follows price … if we enter the market using our 3-day rule, buying when price is above the moving average, as long as the price continues to rise, we theoretically will never need to exit because our sell trigger will only occur if the price falls below the moving average. Now, if the price rises for 30 days, remember the moving average will follow it up, so when weakness occurs and the price finally crosses below the moving average … we exit most likely with a profit since the MA has risen for 30 days following the price. So … a simple sell rule when price crosses below the MA works because the MA is higher and therefore we exit with a profit.

If on the other hand, we enter when price is above the moving average and it quickly changes course and drops below, we find out very quickly that our trade was wrong and we exit, protecting our capital. Since the moving average rises right behind the price, it doesn't take long for a falling price to pierce below the moving average and cause us to exit.

> ***"There are no guarantees in trading – no absolutes. Anyone who tells you otherwise is selling something."*** *- Lindsey Weinger*

This to me is the real beauty of a moving average strategy; the 20-day moving average will never be more than a few percent below the price … so you can never have a situation where you lose 40% as most investors did in 2001. It just isn't possible if you follow the rules, unless of course some catastrophic situation happens like we are attacked by aliens … but in that case, we have bigger problems to deal with anyway.

Think about this a bit … if today the price rises 2%, then the moving average will rise as well, since it is adding that 2% rise to the previous 19 days and finding the average. So as a market changes from an uptrend to a downtrend, the moving average closely trails the price and therefore we don't feel much of the pain of the decline.

> ***"The secret for winning in the stock market does not include being right all the time."*** - *William O'Neil*

If you look at any major decline like late 2012 (Nasdaq chart below), you will see that since the price was rising and the moving average follows the price, at the start of the decline price very quickly crosses the MA. Then as the decline's momentum increases it starts pulling the moving average down with it.

Because price leads the average you will notice that when we are in an uptrend the price mostly stays above a rising MA, whereas when we are in a downtrend the price stays below a declining moving average.

Since the price must stay above the MA for us to stay in a trade, this strategy protects us from a large ongoing drop like in 2001, 2002 and 2003. Conversely, it keeps us in a trade if we have a strong upward move like we did in 1999, 2003 and 2013, since we stay invested until the price falls below the MA.

> ***"Probably my best technique is not picking up the phone to close out a winning trade."*** *- Jerry Parker*

In one sense the techniques we use are similar to a 'buy and hold' when the price is moving in our favor; we will stay invested as long as the market keeps moving up. But as soon as there is a change in the trend, we have protection built into the system that a traditional 'buy and ~~*hold*~~ hope' strategy does not.

> ***"The most important rule of trading is to play great defense, not great offense. Every day I assume every position I have is wrong. I know where my stop risk points are going to be. I do that so I can define my maximum possible draw down. Hopefully, I spend the rest of the day enjoying positions that are going in my direction. If they are going against me, then I have a game plan for getting out."*** - *Paul Tudor Jones*

I spoke about whipsaws already, and this really is the biggest performance killer for a strategy such as ours. If the trend is strongly going up or strongly going down, we enjoy the move, but if it strongly goes up for 5 days, then strongly goes down for 5 days … we end up buying high and selling low. As much as I don't like it, these whipsaws happen and there are ways to minimize the impact many of which we use to protect our client assets at Resnn, but they require much more hands on involvement in order to only invest when there is a verifiable upward trend. The important thing to remember with whipsaws is that although they happen and they hurt when they do, over the long haul you will outperform the market regardless … so you just have to sit through those times and understand why they happen and just bear it.

> ***"If you fear failure, you shall never succeed."*** - *Evan Guay*

Epilogue

> ***"Trading isn't about making hundreds of transactions or jumping on a hot stock. It's about being open-minded enough to realize that we don't know the future – and flexible enough to admit that at some point we might want to trade one position for another. I am a trader because my interest isn't in owning stocks per se, but in making money … I don't have blind faith that stocks will necessarily be higher by the time I'm ready to retire. If history has demonstrated anything, it's that we can't simply put our portfolios on autopilot and expect things to turn out for the best."*** *- Jonathan Hoenig*

As you have seen from the strategy, we use price movement and only price movement to decide whether the market is healthy or not, and as a result whether we want to be risking our portfolio.

We use one item from Technical Analysis to help us gauge the strength of the market, a moving average. Nothing else matters.

> ***"Technical analysis does not have to be complicated. Look at a line on a chart. If it's going up, that's good. If it's going down, that's bad. The problem is that most people can't tell the difference."*** *- John Murphy*

We don't care about the fundamentals (fundamental analysis) of the underlying companies that we are investing in, we don't care about how elevated the market is when we enter (overbought vs. oversold), we don't care whether there is a major catastrophe going on that *should* affect the market, or whether

Jim Cramer or some other *guru* says the market is going up or down, all we are about is how price is holding up.

With all the loads of information available to us, it seems too simple … too good to be true. I mean how can you spend less than 1 minute-a-week and beat 99% of all investors out there? Yet … because of the irrational nature of the market, spending more time doesn't guarantee better performance and it certainly doesn't guarantee you will be protected when the next correction comes around the corner.

Using historical analysis we have created a system that will minimize the risk involved in investing in the market and maximize your return potential in the good years. By using price and price alone, you are easily able to invest in a protective manner since you'll never be invested for long periods of time when a market is in decline.

> ***"Adopt simple rules and stick to them."*** – *Benjamin Graham*

Conclusion

Thank you for Your Time

Hopefully my charts and explanations were self-explanatory. With that said, I have been investing in the markets for a long, long time and what seems obvious to a veteran may be very confusing to others … so I want to encourage you to reach out to me with any questions or comments (my email and website are listed below).

If you haven't figured it out by now, I really enjoy helping people and most importantly empowering people to do it themselves, so I would love to hear from you … no question is a bad one. In fact, as I mentioned many times, I want you to question the status quo … because this is what ultimately brings change.

I also want to encourage constructive criticism. I have spent many years perfecting my craft, but I also appreciate a fresh set of eyes to break apart my analysis. I worked very hard at making certain the data in this book is not flawed, but if you feel there is something that would help the strategy or something I haven't thought of, I would love to hear from you.

Lastly, I have only shown one technique that we employ at Resnn to invest our client funds, our proprietary system is quite advanced and is really in my opinion "the best of all worlds" … geared to maximize the upward moves, while minimizing the downward declines that always come in a business cycle. I strongly feel there is no better way to invest than what we do at Resnn which is why I invest 100% of my personal investable assets identically to how we invest each of our client accounts. I can honestly say I am not only the President; I am also our largest customer as well.

I hope you enjoyed our little jaunt, and most importantly, I hope you feel empowered to manage your own investments. Remember YOU CAN DO THIS; it only takes 1 minute-a-week

… just 20 seconds-a-day. I know it seems daunting, but don't let Wall Street convince you that you can't. You know everything you need to know right now to protect and grow your future into everything you imagined it to be. Invest Smarter …

With warm regards,

Randall Mauro

CEO and Chief Investment Officer

Resnn Investments, LLC

rm@ResnnInvestments.com

www.ResnnInvestments.com

Appendix

Trade Analysis

Listed below are the exact trades over the past 41 years for the moving average strategy. I have included every entry and exit signal along with the profit (or loss) and days in the trade. Although it can be cumbersome to look through this, I encourage you to spend some time looking at each trade to get a feel for the strategy on a day-to-day basis.

Although looking at past results doesn't guarantee the same in the future, it does give you a good feel for what you can expect by using the strategy.

If interested, email me and I will send you a chart of every year of the 41 years listed in the book so you can see visually see every trade that occurred. I find the graphs are very helpful to identify exactly when to enter and exit and to gain a feel for how effective the signals were at timing each trend's move.

20-Day Moving Average Trade Analysis

Starting Value: $10,000.00
Ending Value: $919,152.00

Cumulative Return: 9,091.5%
Average Annual Return (IRR): 11.66%

Total Trades: 188
Average Trades per year: 4.58

Total Days In The Market: 6378 (out of 10,208)
Total Days in the Market Ratio: 62.5%.

Total Wins: 89
Average Win %: 9.57%
Average Win, Days in Trade: 56

Total Losses: 99
Average Loss %: -3.2%
Average Loss, Days in Trade: 14
Largest Loss: -13.2%

Win/Loss Ratio: 47.3%

entry date	entry price	exit date	exit price	+ / -	days in trade	winning trade
7/19/1973	$ 106.52	8/13/1973	$ 104.35	-2.0%	17	
9/6/1973	$ 106.36	10/25/1973	$ 112.31	5.6%	35	1
1/2/1974	$ 92.53	2/6/1974	$ 92.74	0.2%	25	1
3/1/1974	$ 94.05	4/1/1974	$ 91.90	-2.3%	21	
6/10/1974	$ 83.92	6/20/1974	$ 79.85	-4.8%	8	
7/25/1974	$ 73.51	8/1/1974	$ 69.63	-5.3%	5	
10/14/1974	$ 62.04	11/20/1974	$ 60.75	-2.1%	27	
1/6/1975	$ 61.74	4/8/1975	$ 74.53	20.7%	64	1
4/14/1975	$ 77.33	7/25/1975	$ 83.60	8.1%	72	1
10/8/1975	$ 76.61	11/4/1975	$ 76.86	0.3%	19	1
11/14/1975	$ 78.98	12/5/1975	$ 74.72	-5.4%	14	
12/30/1975	$ 76.67	3/18/1976	$ 89.55	16.8%	55	1
3/26/1976	$ 90.89	4/13/1976	$ 88.66	-2.5%	12	
4/23/1976	$ 90.60	5/5/1976	$ 89.24	-1.5%	8	
5/12/1976	$ 90.64	5/18/1976	$ 89.53	-1.2%	4	
6/17/1976	$ 89.72	7/30/1976	$ 91.29	1.7%	30	1
8/13/1976	$ 91.81	8/24/1976	$ 89.13	-2.9%	7	
9/17/1976	$ 91.61	10/4/1976	$ 90.46	-1.3%	11	
11/1/1976	$ 90.39	11/10/1976	$ 87.82	-2.8%	6	
11/23/1976	$ 90.22	1/28/1977	$ 95.72	6.1%	46	1
3/15/1977	$ 96.39	3/28/1977	$ 94.85	-1.6%	9	
4/18/1977	$ 96.17	5/27/1977	$ 96.90	0.8%	29	1
6/15/1977	$ 97.67	8/1/1977	$ 100.76	3.2%	31	1
8/24/1977	$ 100.75	8/30/1977	$ 100.11	-0.6%	4	
9/8/1977	$ 101.28	9/22/1977	$ 99.47	-1.8%	10	
10/5/1977	$ 100.82	10/17/1977	$ 99.14	-1.7%	8	
11/11/1977	$ 100.94	12/22/1977	$ 103.41	2.4%	28	1
12/29/1977	$ 104.42	1/10/1978	$ 99.58	-4.6%	7	
2/2/1978	$ 101.94	3/2/1978	$ 101.71	-0.2%	19	
3/13/1978	$ 103.53	6/23/1978	$ 120.74	16.6%	72	1
7/18/1978	$ 122.09	9/21/1978	$ 132.10	8.2%	46	1
10/12/1978	$ 135.57	10/20/1978	$ 123.82	-8.7%	6	
11/24/1978	$ 116.17	12/20/1978	$ 115.33	-0.7%	18	
12/28/1978	$ 117.30	2/8/1979	$ 123.41	5.2%	29	1
3/22/1979	$ 125.45	3/1/1979	$ 123.33	-1.7%	5	
3/9/1979	$ 127.25	5/9/1979	$ 130.34	2.4%	42	1
5/25/1979	$ 132.68	9/7/1979	$ 148.07	11.6%	72	1
9/17/1979	$ 150.46	10/12/1979	$ 140.71	-6.5%	19	
11/14/1979	$ 137.76	1/7/1980	$ 148.62	7.9%	35	1
1/11/1980	$ 153.87	2/26/1980	$ 158.50	3.0%	31	1
4/14/1980	$ 136.67	10/30/1980	$ 192.51	40.9%	140	1
11/17/1980	$ 203.76	12/10/1980	$ 193.58	-5.0%	16	
12/26/1980	$ 201.28	1/23/1981	$ 197.52	-1.9%	19	
3/3/1981	$ 198.35	5/7/1981	$ 213.66	7.7%	46	1
5/20/1981	$ 217.63	6/19/1981	$ 219.56	0.9%	21	1
8/4/1981	$ 210.09	8/20/1981	$ 207.97	-1.0%	12	
10/7/1981	$ 188.78	12/11/1981	$ 198.64	5.2%	46	1
2/5/1982	$ 188.21	2/11/1982	$ 182.25	-3.2%	4	

entry date	entry price	exit date	exit price	+ / -	days in trade	winning trade
3/25/1982	$ 175.83	5/21/1982	$ 182.40	3.7%	40	1
7/21/1982	$ 171.54	8/2/1982	$ 168.37	-1.8%	8	
8/24/1982	$ 172.23	12/17/1982	$ 228.93	32.9%	81	1
1/7/1983	$ 238.60	7/8/1983	$ 319.57	33.9%	126	1
7/26/1983	$ 320.38	8/1/1983	$ 302.08	-5.7%	4	
9/8/1983	$ 301.79	10/3/1983	$ 294.64	-2.4%	17	
11/16/1983	$ 279.94	12/13/1983	$ 278.92	-0.4%	18	
1/9/1984	$ 287.27	1/26/1984	$ 275.61	-4.1%	13	
4/30/1984	$ 247.44	5/22/1984	$ 240.80	-2.7%	16	
6/25/1984	$ 240.85	7/10/1984	$ 236.25	-1.9%	10	
8/6/1984	$ 249.27	9/12/1984	$ 251.45	0.9%	26	1
9/18/1984	$ 253.99	9/26/1984	$ 250.23	-1.5%	6	
10/23/1984	$ 250.61	11/16/1984	$ 245.12	-2.2%	18	
12/21/1984	$ 244.28	3/11/1985	$ 281.20	15.1%	53	1
4/15/1985	$ 281.07	5/3/1985	$ 280.31	-0.3%	14	
5/14/1985	$ 287.72	6/14/1985	$ 287.95	0.1%	22	1
6/27/1985	$ 295.34	8/8/1985	$ 298.72	1.1%	29	1
10/16/1985	$ 286.68	5/16/1986	$ 384.67	34.2%	147	1
5/28/1986	$ 397.16	7/11/1986	$ 391.55	-1.4%	31	
8/18/1986	$ 379.27	9/9/1986	$ 369.55	-2.6%	15	
10/8/1986	$ 352.90	11/18/1986	$ 352.62	-0.1%	29	
12/5/1986	$ 362.96	12/16/1986	$ 353.77	-2.5%	7	
1/8/1987	$ 377.54	4/2/1987	$ 432.07	14.4%	59	1
5/8/1987	$ 423.17	5/21/1987	$ 408.47	-3.5%	9	
6/8/1987	$ 419.41	9/8/1987	$ 437.60	4.3%	64	1
10/5/1987	$ 453.63	10/13/1987	$ 434.81	-4.1%	6	
12/17/1987	$ 319.51	3/30/1988	$ 371.78	16.4%	71	1
4/1/1988	$ 383.38	4/25/1988	$ 375.27	-2.1%	10	
5/4/1988	$ 381.62	5/12/1988	$ 370.23	-3.0%	6	
6/3/1988	$ 376.86	7/22/1988	$ 387.35	2.8%	33	1
9/9/1988	$ 381.60	10/31/1988	$ 382.46	0.2%	36	1
12/6/1988	$ 377.00	2/27/1989	$ 398.94	5.8%	56	1
3/8/1989	$ 406.40	3/22/1989	$ 400.57	-1.4%	10	
4/4/1989	$ 407.18	6/20/1989	$ 444.58	9.2%	54	1
7/14/1989	$ 448.90	9/20/1989	$ 466.72	4.0%	47	1
10/3/1989	$ 477.28	10/18/1989	$ 463.28	-2.9%	11	
11/28/1989	$ 456.66	12/14/1989	$ 447.48	-2.0%	12	
1/3/1990	$ 460.90	1/16/1990	$ 440.16	-4.5%	9	
2/16/1990	$ 429.01	4/9/1990	$ 430.18	0.3%	35	1
5/9/1990	$ 431.34	6/27/1990	$ 456.89	5.9%	34	1
7/16/1990	$ 469.60	7/23/1990	$ 444.64	-5.3%	5	
11/7/1990	$ 336.80	1/8/1991	$ 359.00	6.6%	41	1
1/22/1991	$ 379.03	4/30/1991	$ 484.72	27.9%	68	1
5/29/1991	$ 499.05	6/14/1991	$ 495.07	-0.8%	12	
7/12/1991	$ 492.71	9/18/1991	$ 518.55	5.2%	47	1
9/24/1991	$ 526.47	10/9/1991	$ 513.81	-2.4%	11	
10/17/1991	$ 536.27	11/20/1991	$ 526.12	-1.9%	24	
12/16/1991	$ 543.73	3/9/1992	$ 615.82	13.3%	57	1

entry date	entry price	exit date	exit price	+ / -	days in trade	winning trade
5/7/1992	$ 587.16	5/19/1992	$ 578.05	-1.6%	8	
6/3/1992	$ 589.93	6/12/1992	$ 569.52	-3.5%	7	
7/14/1992	$ 575.21	8/20/1992	$ 567.86	-1.3%	27	
9/8/1992	$ 571.17	10/6/1992	$ 570.55	-0.1%	20	
10/20/1992	$ 592.70	2/12/1993	$ 690.54	16.5%	80	1
5/6/1993	$ 680.04	6/11/1993	$ 693.19	1.9%	25	1
6/30/1993	$ 703.95	11/8/1993	$ 766.21	8.8%	91	1
12/6/1993	$ 771.09	2/9/1994	$ 786.53	2.0%	46	1
3/9/1994	$ 793.05	3/29/1994	$ 755.29	-4.8%	14	
5/5/1994	$ 740.55	5/13/1994	$ 716.92	-3.2%	6	
5/31/1994	$ 735.19	6/22/1994	$ 712.74	-3.1%	16	
7/18/1994	$ 722.62	9/26/1994	$ 755.63	4.6%	49	1
10/14/1994	$ 767.08	11/25/1994	$ 742.52	-3.2%	29	
12/27/1994	$ 746.19	10/4/1995	$ 1,002.27	34.3%	195	1
10/20/1995	$ 1,039.53	11/24/1995	$ 1,030.17	-0.9%	24	
12/1/1995	$ 1,055.31	12/19/1995	$ 1,026.41	-2.7%	12	
1/25/1996	$ 1,035.95	3/11/1996	$ 1,080.50	4.3%	31	1
3/20/1996	$ 1,101.82	6/11/1996	$ 1,230.76	11.7%	57	1
8/6/1996	$ 1,128.87	10/24/1996	$ 1,227.00	8.7%	56	1
11/11/1996	$ 1,262.67	2/25/1997	$ 1,347.69	6.7%	72	1
5/2/1997	$ 1,305.33	10/27/1997	$ 1,535.09	17.6%	123	1
12/8/1997	$ 1,651.54	12/15/1997	$ 1,536.56	-7.0%	5	
1/6/1998	$ 1,580.14	5/20/1998	$ 1,831.75	15.9%	93	1
6/23/1998	$ 1,844.57	7/29/1998	$ 1,881.49	2.0%	25	1
9/24/1998	$ 1,720.34	10/6/1998	$ 1,510.89	-12.2%	8	
10/21/1998	$ 1,674.75	2/17/1999	$ 2,248.91	34.3%	80	1
3/10/1999	$ 2,406.00	5/26/1999	$ 2,427.18	0.9%	54	1
6/21/1999	$ 2,630.28	7/27/1999	$ 2,679.33	1.9%	25	1
8/18/1999	$ 2,657.73	9/28/1999	$ 2,756.25	3.7%	28	1
10/8/1999	$ 2,886.57	10/19/1999	$ 2,688.18	-6.9%	7	
11/1/1999	$ 2,967.65	4/3/2000	$ 4,223.68	42.3%	106	1
6/6/2000	$ 3,756.37	7/27/2000	$ 3,842.23	2.3%	36	1
8/21/2000	$ 3,953.15	9/13/2000	$ 3,893.89	-1.5%	16	
11/6/2000	$ 3,416.21	11/13/2000	$ 2,966.72	-13.2%	5	
1/17/2001	$ 2,682.78	2/7/2001	$ 2,607.82	-2.8%	15	
4/16/2001	$ 1,909.57	6/1/2001	$ 2,149.44	12.6%	33	1
6/8/2001	$ 2,215.10	6/14/2001	$ 2,044.07	-7.7%	4	
7/3/2001	$ 2,140.80	7/10/2001	$ 1,962.79	-8.3%	4	
8/3/2001	$ 2,066.33	8/13/2001	$ 1,982.25	-4.1%	6	
10/10/2001	$ 1,626.26	1/18/2002	$ 1,930.34	18.7%	69	1
3/7/2002	$ 1,881.63	3/28/2002	$ 1,845.35	-1.9%	15	
5/16/2002	$ 1,730.44	5/31/2002	$ 1,615.73	-6.6%	10	
8/19/2002	$ 1,394.54	9/5/2002	$ 1,251.00	-10.3%	12	
10/16/2002	$ 1,232.42	12/11/2002	$ 1,396.59	13.3%	39	1
1/8/2003	$ 1,401.07	1/23/2003	$ 1,388.27	-0.9%	10	
3/18/2003	$ 1,400.55	8/6/2003	$ 1,652.68	18.0%	98	1
8/20/2003	$ 1,760.54	9/29/2003	$ 1,824.56	3.6%	27	1

entry date	entry price	exit date	exit price	+ / -	days in trade	winning trade
10/7/2003	$ 1,907.85	11/19/2003	$ 1,899.65	-0.4%	31	
12/2/2003	$ 1,980.07	2/2/2004	$ 2,063.15	4.2%	41	1
3/31/2004	$ 1,994.22	4/30/2004	$ 1,920.15	-3.7%	21	
5/28/2004	$ 1,986.74	7/8/2004	$ 1,935.32	-2.6%	26	
8/25/2004	$ 1,860.72	1/7/2005	$ 2,088.61	12.2%	94	1
2/16/2005	$ 2,087.43	3/16/2005	$ 2,015.75	-3.4%	19	
5/9/2005	$ 1,979.67	6/28/2005	$ 2,069.89	4.6%	35	1
7/12/2005	$ 2,143.15	8/15/2005	$ 2,167.04	1.1%	24	1
9/8/2005	$ 2,166.03	9/23/2005	$ 2,116.84	-2.3%	11	
11/2/2005	$ 2,144.31	12/22/2005	$ 2,246.49	4.8%	35	1
1/6/2006	$ 2,305.62	2/7/2006	$ 2,244.96	-2.6%	21	
3/1/2006	$ 2,314.64	5/2/2006	$ 2,309.84	-0.2%	43	
5/9/2006	$ 2,338.25	5/15/2006	$ 2,238.52	-4.3%	4	
7/5/2006	$ 2,153.34	7/13/2006	$ 2,054.11	-4.6%	6	
8/16/2006	$ 2,149.54	12/26/2006	$ 2,413.51	12.3%	91	1
1/16/2007	$ 2,497.78	3/1/2007	$ 2,404.21	-3.7%	31	
3/26/2007	$ 2,455.63	7/30/2007	$ 2,583.28	5.2%	87	1
9/4/2007	$ 2,630.24	11/12/2007	$ 2,584.13	-1.8%	49	
12/7/2007	$ 2,706.16	12/19/2007	$ 2,601.01	-3.9%	8	
12/26/2007	$ 2,724.41	1/7/2008	$ 2,499.46	-8.3%		
3/26/2008	$ 2,324.36	6/11/2008	$ 2,394.01	3.0%	54	1
7/25/2008	$ 2,310.53	9/5/2008	$ 2,255.88	-2.4%	29	
12/10/2008	$ 1,565.48	1/15/2009	$ 1,511.84	-3.4%	24	
2/10/2009	$ 1,524.73	2/19/2009	$ 1,442.82	-5.4%	6	
3/17/2009	$ 1,462.11	6/24/2009	$ 1,792.34	22.6%	69	1
7/17/2009	$ 1,886.61	8/19/2009	$ 1,969.24	4.4%	23	1
8/25/2009	$ 2,024.23	10/30/2009	$ 2,045.11	1.0%	47	1
11/11/2009	$ 2,166.90	1/26/2010	$ 2,203.73	1.7%	50	1
2/19/2010	$ 2,243.87	5/6/2010	$ 2,319.64	3.4%	53	1
6/16/2010	$ 2,305.93	6/28/2010	$ 2,220.65	-3.7%	8	
7/15/2010	$ 2,249.08	8/13/2010	$ 2,173.48	-3.4%	21	
9/8/2010	$ 2,228.87	3/10/2011	$ 2,701.02	21.2%	127	1
3/29/2011	$ 2,756.89	5/18/2011	$ 2,815.00	2.1%	35	1
6/30/2011	$ 2,773.52	8/1/2011	$ 2,744.61	-1.0%	21	
8/31/2011	$ 2,579.46	9/26/2011	$ 2,516.69	-2.4%	17	
10/12/2011	$ 2,604.73	11/19/2011	$ 2,523.14	-3.1%	28	
12/5/2011	$ 2,655.76	4/11/2012	$ 3,016.46	13.6%	87	1
5/1/2012	$ 3,050.44	5/8/2012	$ 2,946.27	-3.4%	5	
6/19/2012	$ 2,929.76	7/25/2012	$ 2,854.24	-2.6%	25	
8/1/2012	$ 2,920.21	10/10/2012	$ 3,051.78	4.5%	49	1
11/27/2012	$ 2,967.79	4/8/2013	$ 3,222.25	8.6%	89	1
4/12/2013	$ 3,294.95	4/19/2013	$ 3,206.06	-2.7%	5	
4/26/2013	$ 3,279.26	6/14/2013	$ 3,423.56	4.4%	34	1
7/3/2013	$ 3,443.67	8/19/2013	$ 3,589.09	4.2%	32	1
9/11/2013	$ 3,725.01	12/31/2013	$ 4,176.59	12.1%	78	1

Addendum

Recommended Reading

For those interested in furthering their knowledge of trading and the stock market, below are some books that helped me on my journey. Good reads for sure, but remember reading more doesn't imply you will perform better... just 1 minute-a-week is all you need ….

How I Made $2,000,000 in the Stock Market *by Nicolas Darvas*

A classic story about a successful trader from the 1950s. There is no doubt that Darvas had some influence on my journey as well as many other great traders including William O'Neil (listed below).

Reminiscences of a Stock Operator *by Edwin Lefèvre*

Another classic published in 1923, which is a thinly disguised biography of Jesse Livermore, a remarkable character who first started speculating in bucket shops at the turn of the century. Livermore, who was banned from these shady operations because of his winning ways, soon moved to Wall Street where he made and lost his fortune several times over. A fun read if you enjoy stock market stories.

How to Make Money In Stocks *by William O'Neil*

If you want to learn to trade individual stocks, all of William O'Neil's products including his Investors' Business Daily newspaper are fabulous, I highly recommend them. I was actually featured in their latest book, *How to Make Money in Stocks Success Stories*, so I'm particularly partial. HTMMIS really helped speed up my learning curve when I was first starting out.

Trading for a Living: Psychology and Trading Tactics *by Alexander Elder*

A fantastic book about trading psychology and getting control of your emotions when trading. His series of books really helped me in my early days.

CHANNEL SURFING *by Michael J. Parsons*

A little known, but fabulous book about trading using Trend Following techniques. This book really made everything crystal clear related to reading a stock chart and understanding the consequences of a particular move on a chart.

EXTRAORDINARY POPULAR DELUSIONS AND THE MADNESS OF CROWDS *by Charles MacKay*

A classic that was written over 100 years ago but still applies today since people's motive for profit and fear of loss has not changed. Not the easiest read, but a fun one that discusses bubbles and euphoria.

SECRETS FOR PROFITING IN BULL AND BEAR MARKETS *by Stan Weinstein*

This book discusses trading using multiple time frames to help discover convergences that can be powerful. He also discusses cycles in the market that help identify when the market is healthy or not.

TECHNICAL ANALYSIS OF THE FINANCIAL MARKETS *by John J. Murphy*

This is really the bible for everything Technical Analysis. More like a text book than a Saturday afternoon light read, but it has literally EVERYTHING related to technical analysis indicators. If you want to tinker with a few strategies yourself, this is worth the cost of the book.

AN IMPORTANT NOTE

The majority of these books did not help me with my trading success at all, so please don't assume that I am giving a thumbs-up to the techniques presented in their pages. With that said, they did help me to understand the markets and the psychology behind how they work.

About the Author

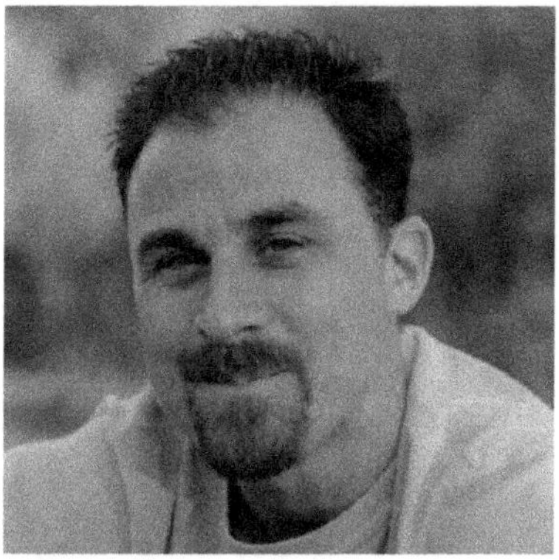

Randall Mauro is the founder and Chief Investment Officer for Resnn Investments. He is a Registered Investment Advisor, registered with the SEC's Financial Industry Regulatory Authority (CRD number: 6105715) as well as the Colorado Division of Securities.

Before founding Resnn Investments, Randall spent 18 years in the software industry as the owner of two Information Technology and Data Analytics firms. The firms took a quantitative data-centric approach to solving various client problems which eventually evolved into the Resnn strategy of using vast amounts of data analysis to deliver solid low-risk performance in both good and bad markets.

Being an outsider to the financial industry made it easy for Randall to identify the problems present in Wall Street today and 'think outside the box' to find alternatives to the status quo. He brings a unique perspective to Resnn … understanding more than most as to what it is like to be a customer of a financial firm and the frustrations that most investors face with typical financial advisors who are more sales driven than performance and value driven.

Want More?

BECAUSE YOU ASKED FOR IT ...

I have received such positive feedback from the release of *Buy and ~~Hold~~ Hope* that I'm excited to say, I am putting the finishing touches on the sequel, *Trust but Verify*. On the next page, I include a free chapter from my upcoming release. I hope you enjoy it…

In *Trust, but Verify*, I provide the tools so that you can invest like the Pros do, whether you want to know how to find a great Investment Advisor to grow your investments, or protect yourself from the bad ones, including details on Bernie Madoff's Ponzi scheme.

I am also happy to say that I include a brand new strategy that actually beats the 20-day moving average technique described in *Buy and ~~Hold~~ Hope*, earning almost 3 times a 'buy and hold' strategy over the past 40+ years again, and, of course, only requiring 1 minute of your time a week. Never again will you be held at the mercy of the market OR any financial advisor.

If interested, please email me at rm@resnnInvestments.com or signup for our *email alerts* at RandallMauro.com to be alerted when the book is officially released.

Trust, but Verify

Death by Shark Bite

ONLY YOU CAN PROTECT YOURSELF

Not much can stop the imagination of a little boy, particularly when his older brother is as adept at scaring the lights out of his bro as my brother was. I remember three particularly *effective* moments when my brother contributed to my now balding scalp by scaring the day lights out of me. These three incidents have become affectionately known in our family as:

> *'Invasion of the Mommy / Daddy Snatchers,' which occurred in 1976*
>
> *The 'Revenge of the Ghosts of All Fish that Little Boys Caught' which occurred in Big Bear, California' in 1980, and of course ...*
>
> *The Infamous 'Catamaran Incident of 1979'*

JAWS; Can you hear the music? Dun, dun, … dun, dun … dun, dun … It's funny to watch the movie *Jaws* today as the shark is pretty fake looking, but many years ago it was a terrifying movie that left the world afraid to enter the water. And the music composed by John Williams is just brilliant! In my previous business I spent a lot of time on the Universal Studios backlot, and remember driving by the Jaws 'pond' late at night and having a chuckle over the story I am about to tell you.

The story is absolutely real, and no, the names have NOT been changed … there were no innocent people in this story. I was 9 years old and my family was visiting relatives at Martha's Vineyard off the coast of Massachusetts. Martha's Vineyard is a sleepy touristy / fishing / beach island. Ironically (for me) … the movie Jaws was filmed there a few years before our visit.

It was a sleepy afternoon and my brother had the brilliant idea that we watch the movie *Jaws* on TV. I remember asking him what Jaws was about and he said it was about "An overprotective clownfish that must leave the safety of his reef and brave the open ocean to rescue his missing son, who is captive in a dentist's aquarium" … ok, ok … I realize in 1979 the movie, *Finding Nemo* had not existed but trust me, my brother did his best work at painting a fun loving friendly fish 'romp' in the ocean. I envisioned a fantastic story, not unlike Flipper and was gung ho on spending the afternoon watching it with him.

It didn't take long before I realized that my brother had upped the ante and quite honestly, he should be proud of his accomplishment with this one. If there was an Academy Award presented to the 'Best Scare by a Big Brother,' he definitely would have won that year.

I remember as the credits were rolling, he dropped the bomb … "Hey Randy, did you know that Jaws was filmed right here in Martha's Vineyard?" He always had a way of carefully waiting for just the right moment to 'educate' me with his incredible knowledge, and it was *ALWAYS* appreciated (I hope you are detecting my use of sarcasm here!!).

It was decided by unanimous decision that Randall would not be going in the ocean again on this trip or ever for that matter. In fact, I had no intention to get in a bathtub ever again after today. I'm not sure how a shark could *get me* in a bathtub, but again, I remind you … the imagination of a 9-year-old is a very powerful thing ~ besides ... Jaws was no ordinary shark!!

You can imagine how I felt later that same day over dinner when my dad announced the 'fantastic' news that we (my dad, my brother and myself) were going "on a little adventure tomorrow. We are going to rent a catamaran and go out in the ocean on it."

To this day I still wonder if my brother had advance knowledge of our plans the next day, he claims it was all coincidence and if it was … man, he must've had the time of his life that evening, but I wonder …

I sat up late that night trying to come up with any excuse to avoid the impending death by shark bite that I was to experience tomorrow. I mean honestly, death by shark bite … could there be a worse way to go???

I'm fairly certain that day I went through all five stages of grief: denial, anger, bargaining, depression and finally acceptance. I remember getting in trouble 'dragging my feet' while getting ready. I was grasping at straws thinking maybe if I got in trouble they would leave me back at the house 'grounded,' while they went to their most certain death.

As we walked up to the rental place, I remember trying desperately one last time to talk my dad out of it … "it looks crowded, maybe we should come back tomorrow," "I think it's too windy," "boy this is expensive, Dad … we don't have to do this," and "I don't know if there's room enough for all three of us, I'll wait on the dock," but ultimately my fate was sealed and we departed on our '3-hour tour.'

I learned after we had departed from the dock as my dad was struggling with the sails that he had never actually piloted a sailboat, let alone a catamaran. As we drifted out to sea, this certainly was setting up for a Perfect Storm. Eventually he got the hang of it and we started moving with great speed through the water. I will say that if I hadn't had the pleasure of watching Steven Spielberg's epic shark movie the day before, I probably would have been digging the moment but given the circumstance, I was terrified.

I remember constantly looking back, expecting to see a shark fin raise out of the water behind us, and every bump of the water on the canvas of the catamaran … I thought for sure was a shark reaching with his jaws to devour me.

Ironically I finally started to calm down, convincing myself that as long as I didn't hear the music, the shark would never come :) … I know it sounds crazy, but again … as I said earlier, the imagination of a little boy can be very compelling.

As I sat and waited for the music to start, the catamaran started tipping up, up, up … and unfortunately I didn't know that this was supposed to happen and started to feel very panicky. Unfortunately, the boat continued to tip and ultimately completely tipped over. I remember the moment so vividly as I slipped across the canvas bottom into the depths of the ocean. Coming up for air, I looked for the boat and saw it about 50 yards away moving very quickly in the opposite direction. Even tipped on its' side, the wind and current was still pushing it along the water at a fast clip. My brother had fallen into the water as well and my dad was hurriedly trying to flip the capsized boat right side up.

I was terrified! If the shark hadn't gotten me while above water, I was now easy prey for his awaiting jaws. I knew that my minutes were numbered …

I remember seeing my dad look at me, seeing the panic in his eyes, trying to control a situation that was out of control. Now as a father, I can only imagine the horror he must have been feeling. Being in the ocean, watching his youngest son drifting further and further away, his oldest son drifting in an opposite direction and a boat that was sinking.

Initially I was desperately trying to get back to the boat but I quickly realized that it was a futile effort. The current was just too strong and I needed to take a different approach. As I saw my father get further and further away, I learned a valuable lesson that day.

My dad, my rock … was not able to get to me. The man that I always relied on for safety couldn't reach me, I had to step up and take care of myself in that moment. In hindsight, I'm actually quite impressed at how that little 9-year-old boy took charge of the situation and *manned-up* to keep himself safe.

Ultimately my father ditched the boat … dove in the water and started swimming toward me. He got to my brother and called out to me to swim toward a deserted island that was reasonably close, which I did. We swam and swam and swam for what seemed like hours and eventually made it to the island and were reunited. The catamaran was gone but we were alive and amazingly Jaws, who was apparently 'asleep at the wheel' missed his prime opportunity to have some tender morsels for lunch.

Having my father so close, but at the same time completely out of reach created an eerie moment, the irony of his close proximity yet he might as well had been over a thousand miles away showed me how ultimately it is you and only you that can protect yourself. Relying on others, even if in this case it was my superhero dad, proved to be a futile effort, and I learned at that moment that **ONLY YOU CAN PROTECT YOURSELF.**

This lesson has carried forward through my years where I know ultimately at the end of the day that I am not only in charge of my destiny but that I am the only one that can keep myself out of a real mess in life. In investing, no one will ever feel the pain of your financial loss as much as you will. An advisor that doesn't protect you properly and steers your investments incorrectly and ultimately causes a loss in your portfolio simply won't be affected by the loss as you will. I'm sure they won't like the situation, but I'm also certain they will sleep fine that night even though they did not protect you from a 30 – 60% loss in portfolio.

In fact, statements like "Past performance does not guarantee future performance" are boiler plate comments that your advisor will tell you or have in the agreement that you sign to try and help soften the blow when and if the above happens.

Ultimately he may have the best intentions, but it is YOU that needs to make certain that all is kosher in his suggested investment mix. If you are going to feel the pain when things go wrong, then you need to verify the decisions he is making on your behalf are prudent. No longer can we assume that this person has your best interest at stake. You need to *Trust, but Verify,* because ultimately when things go terribly wrong it is you that will be alone, all by yourself, treading water deep in the ocean with nothing but a life preserver to keep you alive.

Surrounding yourself with financial advisors and experts in all forms of your professional life makes sense but taking a few precautionary measures along the way, verifying, confirming for yourself that this person is putting you in the proper environments is necessary.

www.ingramcontent.com/pod-product-compliance
Lightning Source LLC
Chambersburg PA
CBHW051651170526
45167CB00001B/423